This Has All Been Wonderful

A Travel Monologue from Summer 1994,
The Year Phish Became Phish

DAVID "ZZYZX" STEINBERG

ISBN: 149756591X
ISBN-13: 978-1497565913

ACKNOWLEDGMENTS

This book would have been significantly harder to write without the incredible work on Phish.net. Having the ability to quickly check song histories and setlists was invaluable. PhishTracks.com was also exceedingly useful for times when I wanted to suddenly listen to every "Makisupa Policeman" in the early 1990s to find out the history of key words.

Thank you, Tom Marshall, for helping me with some research about the names and writing credits of early songs and also encouraging me to actually write about some of my band interactions, rather than just tell those stories in person.

Thanks need to go to my wife Melissa Steinberg, who kept convincing me that people might actually want to read this tome when I was frustrated with the whole process. She also gets much needed credit for driving all the way to Montana over a weekend in late winter to take the photo for the cover. Traveling a ridiculous distance to have a minor adventure is what this book is about after all, so that did seem appropriate.

I'm grateful for the beta readers Ellis Goddard, Melissa (again) and Mary Ann Ingram. Mary Ann gets a special shoutout for being the one to ask me to remove my good jokes and bizarre asides. I still kept some, but she made it a much tighter publication.

The cover design was by Kym Bixler. Unlike me, she actually has a sense of design and can do things beyond the basic Createspace format. The map on the cover is public domain produced by the US Geological Survey.

And of course, thank you, Jon, Mike, Page, and Trey, for giving a depressed graduate student an excuse to leave the heat of southern New Mexico and explore the country for a few months. My life would not be the same without you guys. You might have wished that I had never discovered your band, but you have to go on stage with the fan base you have, not the one you could wish for.

INTRODUCTION

There are towns where you visit and immediately say, "This is the place for me!" Within moments of arriving, you get excited to plan the rest of your life there. That is not what Las Cruces, NM was for a liberal Deadhead in the early 1990s. The homogenization process that first the Interstates and then the Internet created was not yet fully achieved, leading to pockets of regionalization.

The southern New Mexico desert city was very religious and conservative, at least by the standards of a transplant from an extremely liberal northeastern college. In my three years as a graduate student studying mathematics at New Mexico State, I was shocked by many things. There was a gay bashing that led to someone publishing a letter in the student paper that concluded, "Three cheers for the gay bashers." An attempt to close down all Adult Bookstores led to my own adventure in the *Las Cruces Sun News*. I wrote a Swiftian satire in the form of a letter to the editor that used their logic to suggest also closing religious bookstores. Not only did it get some vehement responses, but I learned that there were still people who would catch on that "David Steinberg" was a Jewish name and use that as a springboard to publicly expound some surprisingly anti-Semitic statements.

The modern escape from an incompatible culture was just starting out – which didn't stop me from spending many nights in the computer lab perusing rec.music.phish – but the older approach still existed. Sure, I only made $7200 a year as a graduate assistant but gas was under a dollar a gallon, my three-cylinder Geo Metro managed to get 50 miles to the gallon and concert tickets were cheap. Grocery stores regularly sold cases of soda for $4 and you could get a dollar for each selling them in the parking lot after a show. Most importantly, there was a sense of adventure carrying over from the still extant Grateful Dead scene. Sleeping in rest stops was an allowable form of planning. Truck stop showers were perfect for cleaning up after a ridiculously long night of driving. It might not have been the ideal way for many people to travel, but at the time it was perfect.

The previous summer I had parleyed the time off of school into seeing the majority of the Grateful Dead's tour followed by about 10 Phish concerts. I had the system down, albeit not without a scare or two. I almost ran out of money in Buffalo and had to panic sell nearly 100 Cokes to get to Louisville. Later, on Phish tour, I was evicted from the parking lot in Antioch, TN, for vending and made it back home with about $20 to my name. Rather than scaring me away, the danger and narrow escapes added spice to the adventure. Sure, most of my life was spent trying to figure out Galois Theory and hoping that college undergraduates would appreciate my insights into why business calculus was surprisingly non-horrible, but there was also this secret life where I was living by my wits, trying to figure out where to sleep in strange places. Sometimes I crashed with strangers, others forced me into bizarre options. The quest to discover America: it went from a rite of passage to a cliché to becoming unappreciated again.

Not many would understand why I spent a summer driving around to clubs and theatres seeing a rock band perform, but I wasn't just doing so to escape the delights of summer in the southern New Mexico desert. I slept by the Pacific Ocean and saw cottonwoods shed by Siskiyou Pass. I had an incredibly uncomfortable night in Milwaukee and benefited from the laws of supply and demand in Chicago. A nickname was earned that I would then live to regret. I had adventures that I will remember to my grave. But even beyond that, there was the music. It wouldn't have been enough to have the adventures for their own sake.

That's the hope of this text: to describe what it was like to journey in the pre-Internet age. There will be digressions and road stories and random asides mixed in with the show reviews. It is the combination of music and adventure that makes tour so irresistible. When your favorite songs are mixed with long drives and dramatic events, it gives them that much more power. It feels less like a concert and more like a soundtrack.

Summer 1994 was a magical time, when Phish was first starting to improvise heavily on a regular basis, but still young enough to play their songs with ferocious energy. They were small enough to be able to interact with the crowd after shows, but played with a skill that made it obvious that those days were numbered. By the end of the year, they would play sold out concerts at

Madison Square and Boston Gardens, but that's not how the story starts. Instead, it all began for me at a half-sold club in Dallas, TX.

1: MAY 7, 1994 – THE BOMB FACTORY DALLAS, TX

Saving the best for first.

Around the time I first started seeing the Grateful Dead in 1988, Ticketron and Ticketmaster were fighting for the right to provide ducat availability. Apparently, it was a better image to be the God of Tickets than to bring up memories of a science fiction movie as the Master bought out Tron in 1991. Unfortunately, that buyout brought the end of the best feature that Ticketron offered: I was able to go to Record Theatre in Baltimore in 1990 and casually buy a ticket to a Grateful Dead concert in Louisville, KY. Ticketmaster didn't understand the needs of the subculture that thought it was important to see one or two bands in many different places, so they built an infrastructure that would only allow local buying. As a result getting tickets for this tour was complicated. There were few enough sell outs that it ended up becoming a trivial issue, but it was something that I was worried about before driving the nearly 700 miles between Las Cruces and Dallas.

With many more shows coming up and the end of the semester looming, it might not have been the most intelligent decision to leave at 2 AM on a Saturday morning, drive all day, and go see a concert the same night. Youth has its own logic, and it wanted to see an additional show or two. I just wanted to make sure that the effort would be rewarded. Long distance was not a free service then, but I spent the money to call the venue to see if there were still tickets available. They were non-committal. I figured it would be safe, but I made a few token "I need a ticket" signs and threw them in the back of my car. If nothing else, you never know when those could come in handy when you're about to go on tour.

If you live near the Mexican border, you quickly learn about an obscure detail in Border Patrol law. They have extra powers within 100 miles of an International Border. What they do with that authority is mostly to have

Inspection Checkpoints set up on any major road that winds north. All traffic has to exit the highway and talk to an officer. Usually it is a very straightforward task, but in the middle of the night around (Fine Wine) Van Horn, they can get pretty bored. That leaves things open for a classic game of Harass the Hippie! I was used to being queried about my citizenship, but it didn't stop there. Where was I going? Where did I come from? And most of all, why did I have signs in my hatchback? He spent quite some time questioning me about three pieces of poster board with various Phish-related ticket jokes on them.

The difference between a customs checkpoint and a normal police stop is that the former can ask you what whatever they want and you don't have the same rights. Put yourself in their position: When you're sitting there bored, fantasizing about the medal you could receive for catching a smuggler, anything out of the ordinary is likely to raise flags.

Zzyzx Tour Lesson Number One: *If your journeys are to take you past an Inspection Checkpoint, don't give them a reason to suspect anything is off about you, or you will be there for quite some time.*

I was finally able to explain that I was just trying to get concert tickets, and my journey continued. The stretch between Fort Worth and El Paso is incredibly empty. Large sections of that now have a legal speed limit of 80, but it's not like people drove slower when it was still 65 through those sections. Even my poor Metro was pushed to 85 or so. I was scared that the hamster that powered the engine might die of a heart attack, but it was a trooper.

I arrived at the parking lot to discover that there were plenty of tickets; in fact, the show only ended up being about half to two thirds full. Ticket purchased, I had a different mission. At the time, I was obsessed with an idea I had come up with a year prior. Relistening to *The Man Who Stepped Into*

Yesterday[1], I decided that there was a different interpretation of the characters involved. Tela is accused of being a spy. The story works better if she's innocent and the accusation is evidence that Errand Wolfe is already corrupt. I wrote an essay[2] explaining the idea but the Bomb Factory was my attempt to bring this to a new level. I bought a clipboard and made a mock petition explaining that Tela was being slandered. The idea was to get signatures and then eventually present it to Trey.

What we know now is that the amount of interest a topic has on the Internet bears little relation to how much people at large care about it. The concentrated attention on a subject makes one assume the entire world cares about it as much as you and your friends do. After all, if you're talking about it all day, surely that means that there's a massive groundswell of fascination. Generations of interaction based solely around geographic proximity and accidents of birth made us ill-prepared for a world where we self-select around mutual interests. We still think that our social circles are far more random than they are and that we can generalize from them to populace at large. The above is just a long way of saying that no one in the lot (Such as it was. The parking lot was only large enough for three or four dozen cars and there was no one wandering around trying to sell veggie burritos.) had the slightest interest in signing my petition. I brought the clipboard into the show with me, perhaps with the intent of trying to continue my doomed joke. Instead, I quickly discovered that it served another purpose, that of a setlist table.

I like to keep detailed setlists. It was a process that started when I was seeing the Grateful Dead. It wasn't enough to track the songs. I'd make notes about how they were played. I found myself writing "JFU" (Short for "Jerry Fuck Up" as Garcia's increasingly problematic health issues caused him to stumble his way through shows; at the time we tried to romanticize it as being charming, instead of the disturbing foreshadowing that it was.) as a song note

---

[1] On the off chance that someone picked up this book without knowing this, The Man Who Stepped into Yesterday was Trey's senior thesis. A song cycle set in a fantasy universe named Gamehendge, it contains many of Phish's classic songs. There have been a select few shows where the songs were played in order, with narration between them to explain the story.

[2] Available at http://www.ihoz.com/Tela.html.

quite a bit.

The process escalated in December 1991 when my mom bought me a watch that had a built in stopwatch. Originally out of curiosity, I started timing the length of the sets and writing that down. Eventually that led to timing individual songs. I did this for two reasons. The first is that live music has an intense power. When caught up in a jam, I find myself unable to pay attention to mundane reality like the passage of time. Keeping a watch going lets me know that actually we're just 20 minutes into the set and there's still plenty of music to go. The more important reason is that it's a focusing device. I discovered that I could have a bad tendency to zone out at shows. Keeping a lot of notes prevents one from suddenly snapping out of a train of thought to discover that three songs have passed.

Taking notes though requires a lot of paper. I tried bringing in loose leaf notebooks. They ended up just getting lost. During Spring Tour 1993 I would grab a dozen of the Rift promotional postcards they had at the merchandise booth and use the back of them for notes. They were solid enough to be easy to write on, but they only had them for that one tour. It turned out that the perfect solution was to bring in a clipboard. Decades later I'd still be lugging a sticker festooned piece of particleboard into concerts. Throughout the years I have fielded many questions about what I was gathering signatures for; little did they know that that was the original plan.

Armed with stopwatch, clipboard, and pen, I was ready to take notes. It turned out that it was a good thing I had the space as this is still on the short list of best concerts I have ever seen Phish perform. In fact, if you're – say – writing a book about Phish in 1994 and wanted to do some background research on the Bomb Factory, you'd find out that a majority of the links Google returns for the venue return are about this show.

One thing that gets forgotten about this show is that it had a rather strong first set. There are all sorts of gems lying around that no one ever thinks about. The "Llama" mid instrumental breakdown, the short but very cool surprise jam connecting "Horn" to "Divided Sky," Mike's fun little bass punctuation effects during that song, it all is foreshadowing.

The first sign that this would be anything more than just some playing around the edges happened during "Split Open and Melt." This is an extremely inventive version that builds up to an intense, dark space. Just as it seems about to drop into the coda, there's a detour. The jam gets quieter, leaves the main theme and becomes very Page heavy, leading to a unique ending. In many shows – including quite a few later in this tour when I go on for a bit about the "Melt" - this would be the highlight but this instance was more akin to a stretching exercise. The sprinting would come in the second set.

During the long drive across the Texas desert, I listened to a tape I had just managed to acquire from the previous summer. It was from Tinley Park, IL and centered around a 30 minute "Run Like an Antelope" that had other songs sandwiched in the middle. I wished that we would somehow be receiving something similar in Dallas, but that sort of show didn't come around often. Little did I suspect that the second set would be even more improvisational.

The second set opened up normally enough with "Loving Cup" and "Sparkle" but then it got weird. The "Tweezer" that followed consumed 26 minutes. Just that fact alone was rather shocking for the era. Jams of that length were completely unheard of; even the length of the "Antelope" mentioned above was padded by the mid-jam digressions. Fortunately this wasn't just aimless noodling. There were a few nice build jams and a heavy metal section with Phish singing, "Yeah yeah, yeah yeah yeeeeeah!" on top; I was told that was a Gwar song titled "Gwa" played in honor of the theatric heavy metal band playing next door at the Deep Elum. It was a lie. No such song was teased.

"Tweezer" eventually resolved into "Sparks." This would be my only version of the song until the Dick's "S show."[3] That's too bad because it works really well as a transitional song, filling the space from an end of a jam to the next song inspiration. In this case, it segued into the then rare "Makisupa Policeman." That was a lot of fun but I figured we'd go back to a normal Phish set afterwards. Instead, the end of "Makisupa" morphed into a

[3] Phish played a concert in 2011 where every song's title started with the letter S, providing you pretend there's no "The" in "The Sloth."

Digital Delay Loop Jam. Trey and Mike have unusual tones over the loop; for a few minutes it sounds almost like a Pink Floyd outtake. Then though, it returned to Phish playing a rock and roll styled jam that segued into "Walk Away". OK, surely now we're going to go back to a normal Phish show? Nope, back to the jam. This section was very Page heavy. He plays some beautiful chords for a while over a quiet jam. At one point the music threatened to become "It's Ice", but that was a little too standard for this show. Instead we'd get a one time cover of the Breeders' "Cannonball" because, sure; why not?

Fishman singing "Purple Rain" was almost a relief. The show had been so weird, mixed with intense jams, rarities, and bustouts that it was nice to be able to relax for a second. Don't blow it off too much or you'd miss Jon channeling his Royal Purpleness to scream, "And that means you too, Dallas, Texas!" "Hold Your Head Up" started, but instead of some banter followed by a break, Trey and Fish play the drums together for a while. The jam builds. It considers segueing into "Weekapaug Groove" for a while. Finally, the intro chords to "Tweezer Reprise" are hit and the madness ends, well over an hour after we were asked to step into the Freezer of Coldness.

May 7 was just the first of the twenty-six shows I would see this summer, but it immediately reminded me why I would do something as stupid as drive for twelve hours each way to see a pair of concerts. Sometimes what was shaping up to be an ordinary night of music in a refurbished bomb factory becomes an explosion of a different sort.

In addition to being one of my all time favorite sets to listen to, this night had one more lasting effect on my life. During the extended "Tweezer," the easier to read setlist let me notice how long it was going on for. I occasionally would drop an aside, "We are 50 minutes into 'Tweezer.'" The Greenpeace table staff seemed interested in my chronological updates, so I kept them posted. What I didn't know was that that got back to the band and a nickname was created. From then on, I would be known as The Timer. Yes, the cape was a later invention, but everything else that is known about me - the clipboard, the name - it all comes down to the Bomb Factory.

2: MAY 8, 1994 – THE BACKYARD
BEE CAVE, TX

More about the journey than the destination

No cellphones. No GPS. No ability to tap the source of all knowledge at a moment's notice. It made things a bit more challenging. While the huge venues the Grateful Dead were playing were always helpfully marked on atlases, Phish was still playing clubs. That required some strategy.

One helpful approach in smaller cities was to wander to the downtown area and hope that the music venues were conveniently located there. It's amazing how often that technique paid off. I couldn't ever figure out how to get to the Campus Club due to Providence's confusing one way streets, so I'd just head for the general area and look for a car with Phish stickers to follow. When Phish played The Palace on Vine Street in 1993, I took the Hollywood Boulevard exit off of the 101, because everyone knows that Hollywood and Vine intersect. With all of those tools and history, surely finding The Backyard wouldn't be an issue. The address in the Doniac Schvice[4] was "13101 Highway 71 West, Austin, TX," and 71 intersected I-35. Piece of cake.

There was only one slight problem. The Backyard isn't in Austin. It's in the amazingly named suburb of Bee Cave, Texas. Now it would be difficult to expect people to be able to find Bee Cave on a map, so it made sense to refer to the major city fifteen miles down the road. Still though I spent hours driving up and down Texas 71 getting more and more frustrated, trying to find the place. I'm not sure what inspired me to drive out to Texas Hill Country. I'm a male after all, so I'm pretty sure that I didn't call the phone number. Why do that when you can just drive to random suburbs and hope?

Much like the Bomb Factory, The Backyard is a unique venue that lived up to

---

[4] The Schvice was Phish's newsletter that they send out on actual paper that was delivered by real life mail people. The addresses on the calendar page really were the best way of finding venues. That sounds bizarre to me just typing it.

its name. However they were diametric opposites. Instead of an industrial setting in the middle of the city, one where it looked like munitions could still be made, we were outside in the suburbs in a fenced in area behind a BBQ joint; the coolest part was the home run distance painted on the fence (presumably from the other side of the venue) in case people wanted to start up a game of whiffle ball. The Factory was a few years away from closing its doors whereas The Backyard was only a year old. Unfortunately, there was one more distinction. Instead of a legendary show that is on most people's short list for best show of all time, Bee Cave was treated to a much more pedestrian outing.

That's not to say that there was anything wrong with it per se. This is still 1994 Phish after all. The "Foam" was noticeable – at least by 21st century standards - for just how quiet the instrumental section became. "Stash" has a very cool two-minute digression away from the standard build. It doesn't last for that long but points in the direction of epic versions to come over the next few years (or come to think of it, the next few weeks). And then there's the "Antelope." Taking a best of both worlds approach, it has both a lot of energy and is exploratory in its playing.

If you want to know what makes this era of Phish's playing so special, there's a moment about eleven minutes into the version that sums it up. Trey was playing a very fast lick in order to peak the jam. Mike played a descending pattern underneath it. Suddenly Trey hooked up with it and they played in sync. The jam slowed down and Page jumped on top of it with some beautiful keyboard riffs. Only then were they able to finish the song. It's not just the classic tension and release combination that Phish mined so well in the early years of their career. Having a digression away from the build means that when they return, the fast lick serves both roles – tension for the eventual drop into the reggae part of the jam but the resumption itself is a form of release. This ability is what makes listening to even ordinary shows from this era so fascinating.

After the show, I hopped back in the Metro and started driving back home. I was trying to take advantage of a rule I had learned during road trips on Grateful Dead tour a few years prior. Whenever I was hungry, I would just eat a few bites of French bread and my body would think that I had fed it and it would be satisfied. When tired, I would grab a catnap and wake up refreshed. When you're young, you don't have to eat and you don't have to sleep, you just have to convince your body that you did and it would play along. This only works for a day or two, but there was a break in the tour schedule for me to catch up on my sleep. Sure, there was that whole finals week thing going on, but it's not like that was something important like being too tired to enjoy a show. Unfortunately, there was one problem. It wasn't working. It was getting harder and harder to stay awake. Around Ft. Stockton, I stopped and bought a gas station veggie burrito. As much as I hesitate to call that item "food," after consuming it my energy level doubled. Thus the rule was changed.

Zzyzx Tour Lesson Number Two: *You don't have to eat, you don't have to sleep, but you most definitely do have to do one or the other.*

Walking back to campus on Monday – just because I drove 1400 miles and saw two shows over my weekend doesn't mean that I wouldn't go to class on Monday; ah, to be in my 20s – I found out that there still wasn't a setlist posted for the Bomb Factory. The problem with writing concert reviews in the 21st century is that by the time you get a chance to put finger to keyboard, everyone's heard the show. They've done some sort of live stream during the concert, then downloaded the mp3s, and already had time to form a strong opinion.

Phish.net gets the setlists up – complete with teases and show notes - in something close to real time. I love that existence, but the downside is that there's never a chance to go online and be the one who excitedly gets to inform everyone of what just went down. From leaving Dead shows and reading the shut out crowd the setlist, to finding a computer to give a post show report, to the process a few years later of going to a pay phone and calling the designated Phish net update person with the set, there was always a chance to break Phish news when you saw a concert. Reporting the Bomb Factory details was my Pulitzer.

3: MAY 10, 1994 - PAOLO SOLERI AMPHITHEATER SANTA FE, NM

A day where the sun played tricks.

When you live in the desert, a lot of your day revolves around the sun and how to avoid it. Once May rolls around, whatever you can do to avoid the mid afternoon has to be your goal. There was only one exception to that rule in my three years of living among the cacti: May 10. What made that day so special? There was an annular eclipse.

Despite its name, an annular eclipse is not one that happens every year. Rather it is when the apparent size of the moon is smaller than that of the sun. This causes an effect where the sun looks like a dark circle with a glowing outer edge. Annular in this case comes from the Latin annulus for a little ring. In addition to looking cool through our special projecting viewers, the real effect was to turn down the heat for a welcome change.

The Paolo Soleri show would be Phish's 4th time playing New Mexico since 1991 – 6th if you count the two times they opened for Carlos Santana in 1992. This was a short lived trend. They only played one show ever in the state outside of this four-year period, returning to Las Cruces on 9/22/99. Why did they play the Land of Enchantment so frequently? It's a simple matter of logistics.

If you're playing both Texas and California, there's a giant, nearly unpopulated time zone between the two. Phoenix or Tucson could provide a decent crowd but if you're new to playing out west, it's best to explore all of the markets you can play. The Santa Fe/Albuquerque area has enough of a population that you could get an additional payday to help pay for the gas. Unfortunately, that's only true in theory. When you're not selling out a 650-seat venue as late as 1994, it's not going to inspire you to return too often. Still though, it was definitely appreciated that Phish did play my state all three years I lived there.

If there's one thing you don't expect to see much of driving across the desert, it's rain. Yes it does happen – I ran into a storm in my move to New Mexico and first experienced the fact that desert towns save money by not having a system of gutters. Whenever it rains, every street floods. The worst was the road that I lived on. It was actually concave. Since the shoulders were the high point, after any rainstorm - or even when someone washed their car - a river would pour down the center of the road. – but it's rare enough to be surprising. Breaks from the relentless sun rarely last in New Mexico. El Sol did finally get over its pique over being boxed out by the Moon, leading to a dramatic double rainbow over I-25. This being 1994, I didn't jokingly ask, "What does it mean?" but it's something that stays with you.

With all of the weirdness involving our local G-type main-sequence star, I always assumed that the name of the venue in Santa Fe involved the sun. I never did pick up any Spanish in my three years near the border, so I just quasi-translated Paolo Soleri into "Sun Palace" and assumed that was accurate. Actually, it turns out that that's the name of the architect who designed the venue.

He had an insane utopian image for the place. The idea was that the distinction between the venue and the audience would be diminished, that there would be areas where the performers could wander to be closer to the crowd. The materials were all locally sourced and the hope was that it would be of the desert, not just in the desert. Ultimately it was perhaps too ambitious of a concept for a concert venue. The building was never quite finished and the Santa Fe Indian School – a middle/high school complex that commissioned the venue much to its regret – got sick of the hassles, both of the financial and drunken idiocy varieties, of having it on their campus. In 2010 they decided to close it with the intent of destroying it; as of now though the community is fighting to keep it intact.

None of that was known in 1994. All that we had to do that day was avoid the mud pits (admittedly not exactly at Coventry[5] levels) and enjoy the show.

---

[5] Phish came to the conclusion after a series of disastrous concerts in Vegas in 2004 that it was time to end the band. Their final concert was to be a festival in rural

The concert was a weird backwards show in that the first set had significantly more improvisation than the second. The highlight of the show was the "It's Ice" >[6] "Split Open and Melt", "If I Could" section. Page's solo was exceedingly impressive during the "Ice," hinting at a much faster version of one of his licks in "The Landlady." The "Melt" just was another classic 1994 version.

Certain songs peak in different years. Most of my favorite versions of "David Bowie" hail from 1990. "Possum" was best in 1991-2 when they would extend the introductory section , adding hints and teases. Other than Big Cypress, all of my favorite versions of "Split Open and Melt" occurred in 1994. I'm not one in general who thinks of Phish's playing as being dark or scary. I prefer the soaring uplifting jams that happen in a "Weekapaug Groove" or the peak of a "Slave to the Traffic Light" or the beauty of "Divided Sky," but I'm willing to make exceptions. The dark but still high-energy combination is fascinating enough that I find myself returning to these versions over and over again.

There are two schools of thoughts about going on tour. Some people let the idea of Phish (or the Grateful Dead before them) completely take over their lives. They quit their jobs and see entire tours. There's an actual cult – the infamous Twelve Tribes group famous for handing out psychedelic pamphlets designed to lure in lonelier members of the community - that stalks the Grateful Dead and Phish parking lots with the pitch of, "Tour is great, but what do you do when it's over? Join us and it's like that all the time!" I never wanted to do that. Sure I devoted entire summers to seeing live

---

Vermont. The gods didn't like that idea and sent multiple hurricanes to the region beforehand to make the entire field a quagmire. They had to close down the parking area. People walked up to 20 miles to attend the show, grabbing the bare minimum they needed to survive the weekend. The mud was close to knee deep in spots. My shoes were black by the end of the event, and I had to fly home in socks only because they were so gross that the airline wouldn't let me wear them on the plane. Phish just had to return.

[6] The ">" in a setlist is shorthand for Phish starting the next song without there being any break between the two. If it's a "full arrow" (->), that means the jam at the end of the previous song seamlessly segued into the next. If you ever want to be plunged into the depths of Phish obsessiveness, start an argument among diehards over whether a borderline segue deserves the full arrow or not.

music, but I always had school or a job to return to. My vacation days are largely spent seeing shows, but it will always be part of my life, not all of it. That's why I blew off a Tucson/Tempe/San Diego stretch. I had work to do for a few days but the longer stretch of adventure was almost upon me.

4: MAY 16, 1994 - THE WILTERN THEATRE LOS ANGELES, CA

A theme from the past is revisited

There is one exception to the above rule about never completely going on tour. After I graduated from Bard in December of 1991, I had a little bit of time where I was unsure what I was doing with my life. The first Bush recession made job hunting rough for a newly minted graduate. I had applied to graduate school, but they wouldn't let me in until August. With time to kill, I decided to hit up Dead tour. It started with some stealth shows at the Hampton Coliseum[7], went to the Capitol Centre, and then up to Nassau Coliseum.

For whatever reason Nassau is a cursed venue for me. I was shut out of four Dead shows in my entire life. Two of them have stories behind the inability to attend. At the Boston Garden in 1991, I was a block away from my friend with my ticket but we had no way of contacting each other. The Dead's attempt to skirt the northeast on the 1989 Spring Tour led to severe ticket shortages in the shows closest to the region. I managed to procure tickets to both nights in Pittsburgh, but I gave one away to a woman who needed it more[8]. Those situations were

---

[7] I was exceedingly excited about these shows because of the incredible concerts they had played there in 1989 under the name "Formerly the Warlocks." The rumor had somehow hit Bard about these shows and I really wanted to go to them even though no one was quite sure what they would entail. No one knew if it would even be the Grateful Dead taking the stage or what they would play, but it was exceedingly tempting.

I was just about to drive over the Kingston-Rhinecliff Bridge - an act that would have committed me to attending the show – when I decided that I had tickets to all five Brendan Byrne shows the following week, so I should blow it off. It is still a regret to this day. For the 1992 shows, I drove down to Hampton three different times to get tickets, finally was successful, attended both nights... and they kind of bit. You pays your money and you takes your chances.

[8] She had traveled to The Steel City as a pilgrimage to two friends of hers who were going to attend but had died in a car crash. I helped her look for over an hour and finally just sold her mine. At the worst, I fell for a very good acting job, but if you can stay in

frustrating but understandable. The other two failed attempts stemmed from me going to Long Island.

I eventually gave up getting a ticket for 3/12/92, and retired to a hotel room. Someone I met at the show told me that I could hang out there and get out of the cold. What I didn't know was that they informed dozens of people of that situation. Soon the room became over crowded. There were dogs and someone was trying to set up some drug deals. I figured it was time to get out. I called some friends in Providence and headed up there. Phish would be playing Campus Club the next night. I could resume Dead tour in Philly.

Much to my surprise, Campus Club was sold out. I did manage to find an extra in the lot for face - $10 if you were wondering – and went in. A solid first set anchored by the new songs of "Maze" and "Mound" ended with "Run Like an Antelope." This was to be no ordinary version. Right before the peak, Chris Kuroda turned the lights down to a dark red. The band quieted the jam. The lights came back up and tried to build again, but CK was having none of that. Back to the red and the quieter jamming. Somehow it morphed into their silly power-punk classic "Big Black Furry Creature From Mars." The song is a simple ditty about a boy, an alien, and the bloodlust that conflict creates. However, this night it was never explained, why – oh why - the protagonist wants to kill the listener. Instead, they went into a vocal jam that could have been sponsored by the Hawaiian tourist board. A first attempt to return to "Antelope" got sidetracked, so they sung the second verse of "BBFCFM" at a completely different pace than usual. Then and only then did they end the original song. This was a bizarre jam, especially for the era of 1992 when wild improvisation didn't happen on a regular basis. It had secret language[9] and bizarre jams and a nice peak. Phish would never play Campus

---

character for an hour, you deserve the ticket.. I saw it as a payment to the Ticket Gods that has helped me many times over the years get difficult ducats.

[9] Phish has two kind of secret language. One is a set of signals that was used to clue in the audience to engage in some behavior. For example, if they play the riff from the "Simpson's Theme," everyone is supposed to scream, "D'oh!" There also is a second internal only set of signals that clues the band members as to what to play next. For example, the "Jojo was a man who thought he was a loner" line from The Beatles' "Get Back" means to go back to the previous song/riff you were playing before you got sidetracked. This version of "Antelope" has examples of both. The "Simpsons" signal at the end of the song lead to this being the version featured on

Club again but they definitely went out on a high note.

What does a 1992 show have to do with this story? Well to find out, hop in the Metro with me. Drive out through the desert and spend a night at a rest stop along I-8 that is so isolated that overnight parking is actually encouraged. It can be hard to sleep though because the night sky is so impressive. You can look up from there and see the entire Milky Way galaxy. With no light pollution, you can see the sky in a different way than you normally do. Out in the desert, you get an idea what our distant ancestors saw on a moonless night; the sky feels full of magic. Finally though, sleep does win. There's a plan after all. We need to stop in San Diego to pick up some tickets and then it's off to The Wiltern.

The Wiltern Theatre – named that because it's at the intersection of Wilshire and Western – is an old movie theatre from the 1930s. There was a serious attempt to raze it in the 1970s but a nascent preservation group prevented it from being turned into a parking lot. Instead, the building underwent restoration early 80s and became the stepping stone venue for Los Angeles artists who wanted to get out of clubs. Sure, it might be better known for the fact that Springsteen and Dylan played there, but on May 16, it belonged to a Vermont quartet.

There are many shows that have a signature jam. Fans immediately know what is meant by the "Providence Bowie" (12/29/94) or the "Fleezer" (Finger Lakes Tweezer 6/22/95). To get that status, two things have to be true – the version has to be impressive and it has to be the obvious highlight of the show. The Wiltern "Antelope" shouldn't quite be mentioned along those lines, but it is surprising how forgotten a great version of a popular song in a famous year played in the second biggest city in the country could be. If this book can accomplish one thing, it might remind people that this exists.

Recall that the 3/13/92 "Run Like a Big Black Antelope From Mars" ended with a "Simpsons" signal. The Wiltern had the same cue played early in the introduction. If I thought the band listened to old shows with any regularity, I'd say this was foreshadowing.

---

the episode of The Simpsons' that had Phish's appearance.

The jam almost immediately leaves the standard high-energy build approach that "Antelope" takes. Four minutes into the song, the music quiets. Page takes the lead for a few seconds before Trey and Mike resume control. The energy returns, but it's not the normal theme. Just shy of six minutes in, Trey and Mike start playing the "BBFCFM" introduction. It only lasts for a few seconds, enough to get the dedicated Phish scholars in attendance excited about the call back, but it felt like an abandoned riff. That was a fake out. A minute later, they dive into the song, chanting the first verse. Much like the Providence version, the chorus is eschewed. Instead of a vocal jam, they take this digression as an opportunity to randomly explore. The next thirteen minutes have a reggae styled jam, and a section where Trey and Mike create a floor for Page to lay down beautiful fills that only ends when Trey discovers a stunning theme that he could play. Just when it seems like no one will remember what song was being played, Fishman picks up the pace, and the "Antelope" jam reemerges. There's an extra advantage to drawn out versions. The peak jamming sounds even faster when your ear has readjusted to the slower improvisation of the jam. How far out did this go? When Trey finally gets to the "Rye Rye Rocco," lyric, he first chants, "Set the gearshift for the high…" to that tempo before catching himself and laughing.

Which "Run Like a > Big Black Furry > Antelope" is better? There really isn't a question. 1992's version had a much stronger element of surprise going for it and the jam is a lot more fun. Los Angeles did have one variant of the game. The "Creature" returned later in the set.

While the set had mostly returned to normal 1994 parameters, the earlier exploration colored the music. "You Enjoy Myself" had a full band tease of "Louie Louie" towards the end. Perhaps that moment was when they realized they were still wanting to have fun with setlists. "YEM" was followed by revisiting "Big Black Furry Creature from Mars." This "Creature" feature was more of a remake rather than a sequel. The first two verses were sung again, complete with chorus this time. A full version of "BBFCFM" usually contains a pause towards the end. This night they took that time to sing "Amazing Grace." Did that mean that the Creature itself was once lost and now is found? Maybe not. "1-2-3-4!" was screamed and Mike exclaimed that he was running, running from you.

Perhaps the band was trying to teach us a lesson. Even a scary Martian could experience redemption and it could be foolish to be terrified of them before discerning the status of their soul. It could just be the sharp relief that contrasting a punk rock song about inflicting violence with an a Capella, unamplified call for salvation. Even if the "Wilternlope" is reprise instead of an invention, these thorny moral issues - ones that are completely not a case of me reading way too much into a setlist, really - are a reason why this show should get more attention than the current none that it receives.

5: MAY 17, 1994 – THE ARLINGTON THEATRE SANTA BARBARA, CA

A brief history of Page birthday shows in the 1990s

Much like the previous show, 5/17/94 was a flashback to a series of events that started at Campus Club, only this time I knew it was coming. It began in May of 1991. I had an urge to visit some friends in Providence and get off campus for a few days. So I did what I always do. Phish is playing Providence and I can spend some time with Sue and Kathy? Cool! It's a two-fer!

It looked at first like this plan was going to backfire. Midway through the show opening "Chalk Dust Torture," there was a blackout. This was shaping up to be the shortest concert in the history of Phish. After leaving the stage for a few minutes, they brought out their secret weapon. Carl "Gears" Gerhard was in the venue – perhaps he was rehearsing for the Giant Country Horns tour that would be happening the following summer – and Jon and him came out and played a drums/trumpet duet. This evolved into a cover of John Coltrane's "Mr. P.C."[10] The "Spiderman Theme" solo Gears plays on this track makes this moment worth a listen. Even the gods of electricity agreed as power was restored and the show went back to being a normal late club period show.

The first time I had any idea it was Page's birthday came before "The Man Who Stepped into Yesterday." Trey went on a mini rant on the theme that Page was so old – an outright ancient 28! – and introduced the song as "The Old Man Who Stepped in Yesterday." Those were the two themes of

---

[10] In modern terms, one might think that a Mr. P.C. would either be someone really into computers or who always used the perfect phrase to refer to disadvantaged groups. In this case though, it was praising the efforts of the bassist on the track: Paul Chambers.

the show: Page was to be wished a happy birthday and Gearhard would play on occasion. Both "Fluffhead" and "Big Black Furry Creature From Mars" had breaks to sing "Happy Birthday" to Page. Meanwhile, Gears had great solos on the jazz classics. He also came out to play on "Cavern," but didn't quite ever play the fill that the Giant Country Horns would bring to the song that summer.

Many 1991 shows can blend together. They were all fun and worth the $10 or so that they cost, but few actively stand out. Between the fun "Flintstones Theme" jam in "Caravan," and Fishman singing, "How old are you?/ How old are you?/I'll tell you how old he is! 1-2-3-4!" as a way to return to "BBFCFM," this is a definite exception. If you're in the mood for this time period, this show is highly recommended.

Based on the official tour calendar, Page's 29th birthday would be uncelebrated. Instead though, they took an idea from the In and Out Burger playbook and had a somewhat secret show. Attendees of the Capitol Theatre show a few days prior, were informed that there would be a concert on the 17th in Schenectady. I had never been to Schenectady but I sure loved saying it. With no other plans, it was worth a trip.

Even before the music started 5/17/92 was notable for being one of the last $5 shows. Maybe it was the Union College affiliation or perhaps it was the last second nature of the event, but that's a pretty unimaginable ticket price[11]. At that price, the most standard show ever would easily have been worth it, but this was one of the better shows of the year. There was a great "Colonel Forbin's Ascent;" the story section of that song was just starting to get weird in 1992 and this is a great early example. The floor becomes a sheet of ice. It starts to tilt and we slide off into space until we slowly float into Gamehendge. There's even a joke on sound man Paul Langluedoc's nickname. As Forbin was climbing, he was grabbing onto roots, grabbing onto roots, he was grabbing onto the Root Doc! Good thing Paul got transported with the rest of us, or the revolution would have been much less successful.

---

[11] Mind you, that wasn't the cheapest ticket price I have seen. That would be either 5/10/92 or 9/16/90, both of which were free shows on college campuses. "What about Amy's Farm?" you ask. That was technically a free show but Amy asked for $5 parking money to recover the costs to repair the damage to the field.

The musical highlight of this show is clearly the "Possum." Most of my favorite versions of the ditty about roadkill come from late 91/early 92 where the introductions were long and weird. This was a classic rock tease extravaganza. It started out when Trey stumbled across the riff of "Rocky Mountain Way." It quickly became a full band jam on the theme. That was followed by a "L.A. Woman" jam.

Want to know the secret of Phish's success? Check out how fast Mike catches onto what Trey is playing. By the second chord of the riff, there's already bass accompaniment. This isn't a one-time fluke. As the first verse ends, Trey veers into "China Grove" and the rest of the band is playing along almost immediately.

This is a reason why the slow growth was so important. The listening and playing off of each other in 1992 is what made the extended jamming of 1994 possible. You can take chances in front of a small crowd and see what works. Jamming was a hit. Secret Language really only had a shot in the clubs and theatres when there was a more critical mass of fan. The anti-song that was "Wait" [12] was quickly discarded. The years in the clubs were crucial to letting Phish learn the skills that would lead to them breaking out of those venues.

Another reason why Phish is still so successful is their sense of humor. In the midst of teasing all of those huge hits, Trey also managed to smuggle in references to some of their own songs; both "It's Ice" and "Divided Sky" were teased. Much like The Beastie Boys sampling themselves in "Johnny Ryall," it shows confidence in the song catalog, but does so in a way that's flip instead of egotistical.

When it comes to humor, the best sections usually are when Fishman comes up to play the vacuum. After mocking Page for playing "Happy Birthday" to himself, Jon takes a lot of time giving the ages and birthdays of the band… and then the crew… Finally Trey ended it with the slogan, "Phish: more entertainment for your entertainment dollar!" Somehow that failed to

---

[12] "Wait" was a joke where they would play a riff, say, 'Wait," like they had messed it up, and then play it again… and again… and again some more. They did this for so long on 10/31/90, that the crowd chanted, "Fuck you!" back every time Phish said, "Wait."

make it onto t-shirts.

With less ubiquitous tapes, one time could be forgotten. Twice is more difficult. Two fun Page birthday shows set a pattern. In this case though, it wasn't the music that was most memorable; it was the venue. The Arlington Theatre is perhaps the most surreal venue I have ever attended.[13] The inside of the building is designed to look like you're in the plaza of a Spanish village. There are facades of houses along the side walls, complete with balconies. The illusion is very hard to shake.

Sure I spent most of the night staring at the walls and pretending I was in Europe or Mexico, but there are some notable highlights from the show. The "Maze," complete with the inevitable "Happy Birthday" tease, is especially strong. There's also the "Tweezer" that becomes a cover of Cheech and Chong's "Earache My Eye," if you're paying a lot of attention and can hear Fishman's vocals buried deep in the mix. Like so many things, Page birthday shows were a lot more fascinating when he was in his 20s.

---

[13] One exception might be the Greenfield Armory Castle on 12/5/91. It was an actual armory and had a sign up about what to do in case of nuclear war. It wasn't a duck and cover type response. It detailed how to counterattack.

6: MAY 19, 1994 –
HULT CENTER FOR THE PERFORMING ARTS
EUGENE, OR

A trip up the coast is rewarded with a "Stash"

It's nearly 900 miles along US 101 and Interstate 5 to get to Eugene from Santa Barbara so the west coast was treated to its first off day of the run. Personally I was excited, as San Francisco was the furthest north I had ever wandered on the west coast. I was exploring new ground.

I woke up the morning of the 20th at a state run campground in California along the coast. There were tons of these in the mid 90s. They charged a nominal fee and had very nice showers, so they were perfect for the touring crowd… which I'm pretty sure basically meant me on this stretch of the road; it would pick up more after the break.

101 is a rebel highway. Its number doesn't confirm to the usual rules that apply to three digit highways, as it is not a spur route off of the East Coast's US 1. It cedes the shore to the Pacific Coast Highway until the Bay Area, but then it hugs it all the way to Washington State. It circles all the way around the Olympic Peninsula, which gives it the oddity of having it flip directions as you continue to drive. If you go to the end of US 101, you will be following the lines going south, regardless of which end you are hitting.

If I had known this route the way I do now, I probably would have stuck with the coastal route past Crescent City and cut over to I-5 in southern Oregon. Instead I cut across the east Bay and took 580. While that's a much more treacherous road if you're not used to it, full of endless miles of mountain passes, it was worth it for two reasons. One is that I got to see endless signs for Manteca, CA. While Phish cover a lot of songs in concert,

Dizzy Gillespie's "Manteca" is the rare non-original to make it onto a studio album. I sang, "Crab in my shoemouth," every time I saw one. However, that was the dumb reason. The true advantage is that you drive by Mt. Shasta.

Rising to 14,179 feet above sea level and nearly 10,000 feet above the surrounding valley, Mt. Shasta is visible over 100 miles away from its peak. While I had seen mountains in New Mexico and Colorado, this was my first time seeing a 14er from a floor that was below sea level. This is one of the reasons why tour was so amazing in the mid 90s. Modern Phish tour focuses mainly on big venues in major cities. In the 90s, shows could be almost anywhere. As stunning as Mt. Shasta is, it's almost a forgotten peak with all of the National Parks that California has. Sure sometimes Phish brought me to Kalamazoo and Kansas City, KS, but that moment of first seeing Shasta – along with stopping at a rest stop in southern Oregon the next day, eating a cold can of ravioli (tour cuisine at its finest!) while watching cottonwoods shed white fluffy strands: the mountain air made me feel like the Pevensies in Narnia, like I could run for miles without getting tired - will stick with me always.

Zzyzx Tour Lesson Number Three: *Sometimes it's not about the show or the people or the venue, but rather about the places you see that you would never have experienced in a million years. This is a vast and amazing country and some of the best places aren't on the usual tourist trail. Go to the weird shows in the strange places and who knows what you will discover.*

Even if you ignore the fact that it's in the extremely cool small town of Eugene, the Hult Center has two things going for it. It is a mere half-mile from Eugene's amazing Keystone Café and the roof of the venue is intriguing. It has interwoven wood panels akin to that of a wicker basket. Perhaps it was created that way to improve the acoustics of the Silva Concert Hall or maybe it was an economic decision. They were under some budgetary constraints as the venue was paid for largely by a bond measure on Eugene residents. It had already failed in two previous votes, so they were likely to be more aware of the need to keep funding under control. Regardless of the reason, it was hard to pay attention to the band as looking at the ceiling was a constant distraction.

Distractions or not, the band did come out to play two sets. For the most part, this show is a completely standard concert for the era. There's a reason even diehard Phish fans don't reference this night often. With so many incredible concerts around this, Eugene can be overlooked. It's a classic example of what I call the Idaho Effect. Idaho has 12,000 foot mountains, incredible waterfalls, cool bridges, and stunning lakes. The only problem is that it borders on Montana, Wyoming, and Utah. As a result, its delights tend to get ignored, as it is the state that you drive to on the way to get to the really incredible ones. A vacation in Idaho feels a bit like a consolation prize but if it were anywhere else in the country, it would be the destination. If you take a break from the usual suspects of 1994 and put in May 19, you might be quite surprised by what it contains.

Taken in isolation, this show has three things going for it. The first is simply that Phish was much younger then and played with an energy that can be shocking if you have been listening to a diet of 1997 or 2004 era shows. Sure that's true of most of 1994 but it still can impress. Just listening to this show could possibly de-age you, at least for the duration you have it playing. There also is an amusing thematic element from the night. Trey plays the theme to *I Love Lucy* during "Weekapaug Groove" and then again in the introduction to "Harry Hood." Between the two is the quasi-song of "Big Ball Jam" and that's where Lucille's influence is most welcome.

"Big Ball Jam" was a game that only could be played in small venues. Three large rubber balls were thrown out in the crowd. Each one corresponded to a non-drumming band member. While Fishman kept up a steady drumbeat, the other band members would play a chord if and only if an audience member was touching their ball. [14] It would go on for a few minutes and then Trey, Mike, and road manager Brad Sands would join hands to form a giant ring. The game would then be to try to throw the ball into the hoop. Not only was that fun, but once all three baskets were created, they'd go on and play a

[14] Yes, yes, touching their ball. The jokes have all been made many, many times. Let's let it pass, OK?

different song. "Big Ball Jam" was usually fun in the moment but on tape it sounds like "Plink. Plunk. Plink. Do-doot-do-doot-do-doot (audience member shaking the ball fast). Plunk etc. etc." In this version, every time Trey's was touched, he'd play the next chord from *I Love Lucy* theme. The actual melody involved makes this version listenable after the fact. It worked so well that that two nights later, this idea would be reprised with the famous riff from "Smoke on the Water."

Teases are fun but can be a bit gimmicky. That complaint cannot be levied against the "Stash." I've seen the song 84 times and this is either my favorite or second favorite version. The jam is intense, dark, fast, and loud. They experiment with this style many times in 1994, but this is a quintessential example. Do not operate heavy machinery while under the influence of this Stash, lest you find yourself driving 110 in traffic… or somehow become transported to a scarier universe.

Should you immediately run out and download a copy of Eugene? I wouldn't suggest that anymore than I'd push for a trip to Boise. However, if you happened to find yourself listening to it, you'd be in for quite a few treats.

7: MAY 20, 1994 -
CAMPUS RECREATION CENTER
THE EVERGREEN STATE COLLEGE
OLYMPIA, WA

Ob La Di, Ob La Da, Geoducks go on.

The Evergreen State College is an experimental university. Students don't receive grades there; teachers describe each student's performance in an essay. It has an organic farm and classes with titles like, "Activism, Advocacy and Citizenship," "Approaches to Sustainability," and the distinctively punctuated, "Can Science Help Me? ... To Be Better?" The school mascot is the geoduck (pronounced "gooey-duck" for reasons I have never been able to figure out), a local clam that has a rather pornographic appearance. It's located in Olympia, which is on the very edge of the Seattle liberal bubble.

Washington gets thought of as a blue state, but it's really an extremely liberal, populated area surrounded by sparse conservative territory. Evergreen is where it starts to mix, which can lead to occasional conflict. While it since has moved further south, there used to be a billboard not far from campus that had a giant picture of Uncle Sam with room for an ever-changing conservative message. Once it said, "Evergreen State College – home of environmental terrorists and homos?" The school used to sell a postcard of that message, which shows that they aren't sucked so far into their bubble to not be able to laugh at themselves.

Phish played Evergreen State College four times. Their final performance in November of 1994 was a rather legendary show that later got released in the Live Phish series. However, I would be back in New Mexico for that performance. It was the penultimate Evergreen show that I was heading for, on my first day ever in Washington State.

If you're a road geek like me – and odds are that you aren't, but work with me here – each time you enter a new state, it's a chance to see how a different region chooses to represent itself. Oregon refuses to put the word "Limit" in their speed limit signs. Pennsylvania and California pretend that no other states exist. It's amusing to see I-80 tell you that it's the road to Stroudsburg and Delaware Water Gap instead of New York City or to have I-10 regulate Phoenix to, "Indio Other Desert Cities." Indiana used to tell knock knock jokes in construction zones.[15] Most fun are the state route signs. Sure many are just a square or a circle with a number inside; if they were feeling inventive, maybe they'd put the outline of the state on the marker. Some though are creative. Kansas uses a sunflower. Utah has a beehive. Most amusing though is the Evergreen State. The last thing I was expecting to see as I crossed the Columbia River was a silhouette of George Washington's head. Who says massive government bureaucracies can't be funny?

I had some pretensions of being a taper during this era. Other people had elaborate rigs and expensive pieces of equipment. That wasn't my approach. I had the worst deck in the section, purchased on a whim at a Las Cruces pawnshop for $40. It recorded in mono. Its heads were slightly out of alignment so I had to record a second copy off of the master onto a different deck, because it only ever played back correctly on itself. Whenever the tape counter[16] got to a new hundred mark, the play button would pop out. I had to

---

[15] I saw this along I-65 on the Grateful Dead's 1993 Summer Tour between Louisville and Chicago. They had a sign up every mile of the construction zone telling you that you were making progress then will three miles left, the sign said, "Knock Knock." I – of course – said "Who's there?" to the air. Next sign, "Orange." The punchline: "Orange you glad you only have a mile to go?" I never claimed it was a funny knock knock joke.

[16] To be honest, I never quite understood what the point of a tape counter was. For those in the digital era, analog tape decks had a spinning numerical readout that incremented as the tape played from 0 to 999. However it didn't correspond to any sort of time or feet of tape measurement. In the best-case scenario, they could give you some idea of how much tape you had left on the side, but it was a pretty vague estimate.

How hard is it to figure out what these mean? Investigating found an article in *The American Mathematical Monthly* (http://www.maa.org/pubs/calc_articles/ma062.pdf)

keep an eye on it and hit the reset button whenever it got into the 90s. Eventually I just duct taped the button down and that solved the problem.

Like a 16 year old with a broken down car, I romanticized the hell out of the foibles. I didn't tape often – the price of batteries and blanks prevented that – but there weren't many tapers on the western run. I knew I would be waiting for months or years to hear these shows again unless I taped them myself. So I stopped at a Kmart in Centralia, WA to purchase supplies.

There was an unusual device in the electronics department – a video kiosk. This was still the era of MTV. Music videos were important. With no Youtube, the closest thing to video on demand was to go to the Kmart and watch it there. Oddly enough, the "Down With Disease" video was an option. I queued it up and enjoyed. Sure it cut off halfway through – more like "vid o dema" than video on demand – but that was my only time getting to see it for decades, at least without snarky commentary overlaid on top.

Like so many shows of this era, the first set was so high energy that you could strap a generator to Trey's fingers and power a medium sized city. Bringing back memories of the Paolo Soleri performance, the "If I Could," "It's Ice," section really stood out, but the highlight was in the second set. It was another flashback, this time to a show I didn't attend. The lesson taught here is about the danger of narrative.

There are people who swear by audience recordings and eschew official releases. They prefer the more "organic" recordings where you can hear the audience. I've even heard the derisive term "sound bored," for board tapes. Normally I'm not one of them. I prefer to hear the music, not the crowd. 5/6/93 is an exception though. Trey starts playing "Ob-La-Di Ob-La-Da" in the middle of a "Mike's Song" and the audience goes absolutely bonkers. The majority of the song is played as an instrumental that becomes a loud sing-along on the choruses. I listened to this tape quite a few times that year, largely because it was one of those moments where the band and crowd perfectly synched up.

---

that used some rather elaborate formulae to try to generate meaning from this indicator. Ultimately they have to punt concluding, "A stopwatch might also be used for more careful estimates." The Timer approves of that sentiment.

Syncing is not what was happening at Evergreen State. The audience – at least where I was standing – seemed distracted and disinterested. The show was really good from the start; the "Bathtub Gin" in particular is high energy and has a quick "The Lion Sleeps Tonight" tease. It sounds like the versions that they're trying to play in 3.0[17] only much stronger. Despite that, the crowd seemed more interested in their conversations. Phish needed to use the nuclear option. Late in the second set, they pulled the "Ob-La-Di Jam" card out during "You Enjoy Myself." The crowd went blasé. Shortly after that, the song (and the show) ended. This group apparently didn't deserve a Phish show if they're going to ignore the ultimate weapon.

At least that's the story I told myself. I finally relistened to this show years later and none of that was apparent. The crowd noise wasn't louder than normal and the reaction to songs and teases showed that they were indeed paying attention. For that matter, it definitely doesn't explain the very fun "Low Rider" jam in the vocal jam section of "YEM." An annoyed band wouldn't do that.

Zzyzx Tour Lesson Number Four: *Just because you can build a narrative in your head, doesn't mean it's actually happening. People like to talk about crowd energy. Shows are sometimes juxtaposed based on how engaged the audience was. Frequently, these stories about crowd energy really are referendums of how the dozen or so people around you are behaving that should not be generalized to the crowd at whole. It can be fun to create tales, but don't assume that they're universal.*

---

[17] Phish fan shorthand. Phish 1.0 is 1983-2000. Then they took a break for a few years. 2.0 was 2002-2004. Then they left forever and ever and ever, aka 5 years. 3.0 is 2009 – indefinite as of time of writing.

8: MAY 21, 1994 – THE MOORE THEATRE
SEATTLE, WA

Found a city, found myself a city to live in.

Seattle is a mere 70 miles up the road from Evergreen. As of this writing Phish haven't played anywhere in the entire Pacific Northwest region other than The Gorge (a stunning venue, but also one located 3-5 hours away from the populated parts of Washington and Oregon) in fourteen years, making this run of cities and small towns somewhat surreal to revisit. The small trips could be challenging – when living on the road, having long drives every day gives you something to do – but I had a place to crash in Seattle's University District via a connection made on rec.music.phish, and I was about to receive a tour of the Emerald City.

For some reason, I have always had an affinity for Seattle. I wore a Mariners hat throughout the late 80s and early 90s for no apparent reason. My first choice for graduate school was the University of Washington. I had never seen the town and knew nothing about it, but was fascinated by its existence. I had finally arrived. Seattle would not disappoint, as it was U District Street Fair weekend.

The one advantage of Seattle's rainy climate is that people really celebrate when it's gone. A sunny and warm day in the New Mexico desert is normal, but when clouds and chill are the default, everyone gets excited on that first 70 degree, stunning day. Walking up and down "The Ave" showed an energy that existed few places. Especially coming from a town whose populace was in a never-ending battle against heat exhaustion, one where summer siestas weren't laziness, but rather were a form of resistance against the constant, oppressive heat, Seattle seemed to crackle.

1994 was a transitional year for Seattle as much as Phish. Grunge was evolving into software dominance, which meant that there was starting to be money but there still were musicians wandering everywhere. It felt like a band was forming on every street corner. Seattle summer days are evil. The sun makes everything incredibly green causing people to move there, thinking it might always be like that. Then the endless rains of November arrive... That's later though. On this day I was completely smitten; I would move in under a year.

The Moore Theatre is surprisingly old for a Seattle venue. Seattle was first founded in the mid 19th century. All of downtown burned down in 1889 and had to be rebuilt. This led to construction jobs; between this and the shipping jobs inspired by the Alaskan gold rush, the city grew quickly. Perhaps it was this influx that caused the need for a quality theatre a mere 18 years later. The boom/bust cycle of Jet City – even after the gold rush years, Seattle rode Boeing to prosperity, fell in the 70s when the company had some lean years, and then had a resurgence when an obscure software company in Redmond created a product called Windows - causes a constant reinvention. Buildings are being torn down and recreated. Not even the land is immune. As hilly as Seattle is now, this is the after following decades of construction projects to flatten things out. Buildings might be destroyed, the landscape could change, but the Moore Theatre remained in Belltown, immune to the changes around it.

If there's one thing that Phish fans thrive on, it's change. Trey has commented in interviews about how it keeps them on their toes. They can't just casually repeat a joke that was made a few months ago, because there will be someone there who was at both shows or who has the other night on tape and will lament, "Really? This joke again?" That attitude has made them a better band, but we might be happier as a community if we were able to appreciate some repetition. A jam of incredible beauty could be played at a show, one that brings everyone to rapture, but if it were repeated a few shows later, euphoria would become ennui. [18] I was reminded of this while listening to "Down With Disease."

On the New Year's Eve prior at the Worcester Centrum, Phish performed

---

[18] A great recent (as of time of writing) example of this happened in summer 2013. During pauses in the Lake Tahoe "Tweezer", fans spontaneously started chanting "Woooo!" This led the band to play an absolutely stunning, high energy jam. When a "Woooo!" shout started at the next show, there were already grumblings that it was getting old. One show was all it took to jadeify.

their first real stunt. The tour was played in a giant aquarium set complete with plants and a giant clam. Four people – supposedly the band members – in diving suits were slowly suspended down to the stage. Then the clam acted like a puppet. It slowly, slowly, slowly counted down from 10 – the actual countdown takes close to a minute and cracks me up every time. "Teeeeeeeeeeeeeeeeeeeeeeeeeeeen" [long pause] "Niiiiiiiiiiiiiiiiiiine" – leading into 1994. The first song of the year (well other than "Auld Lang Syne")? No one knew it. It was this incredibly upbeat instrumental, one of the happiest things I had ever heard.

Eventually we found out that it was the jam section to "Down With Disease." That was an appropriate title, I thought, because this jam is so amazing that it's likely to be able to cure diseases. How long did being completely thrilled by that jam last? Three performances. In the next couple of years, "Down With Disease" would usually contain a long improvisational section out of the happiest riff ever – and I still think that if I wrote that song, I would spend all day playing it over and over again, just because I could – and I learned to love it again, but it shouldn't require that. Losing interest that quickly is a failing of ours.

To the degree that this show is remembered and talked about, the conversation largely focuses around a spontaneous joke in the second set. After the ever-popular Fishman vacuum song section[19], people called out requests. A running joke over the years is that it's impossible for the band to

---

[19] Jon Fishman, "the second best trombonist drummer in all of Vermont," has a second role in the band as a surreal frontman, Trey mans the drum kit and the rest of the band plays "Hold Your Held Up" (chosen because Fish loathes the song) as Jon takes center stage. Usually clad in a dress (OK, a "frock") covered with orange donuts, he grabs an Electrolux vacuum cleaner, and sings a bizarre cover; Syd Barrett era Pink Floyd songs are especially popular. Halfway through, he turns on the cleaner, puts his mouth next to it, and uses the suction to create an unnerving sound. Sometimes he can get actual melodies out of it. The vacuum section doesn't happen often these days; it usually signifies that the band is in a silly or talkative mood. Some fans love it, others hate.

The best reaction to the vacuum songs - of course - was Mike's. On the cusp of Phish's big forever breakup in 2004, Trey asked the other band members if they thought the Fishman section made or ruined a show. Mike's response was, "On a scale of 2 to 3, I give it a 3."

decipher when hundreds or thousands of people are calling out for different tunes. After playing with that joke for a while, there was a twist. Trey suddenly announced, "We'd like to give you guys the opportunity. We've been playing for you all night. We'd now like to give you the opportunity to play for us. Ladies and gentlemen 1-2-3." After being counted out, we did our best. It doesn't come out well on the tape that circulates, but people clapped to make a drum beat and then cheered to create some melody line.

There's a term in French, "l'esprit d'escalier" (literally "the wit of the staircase") that expresses that moment of frustration when you come up with the perfect joke or retort only after the moment has passed. If there's an opposite term, that would apply to this moment. For after we finished "playing," Fishman said, "Oh man, you guys haven't played that in so long!" It was the perfect mockery of our quest for uniqueness over quality. Like Robert Pirsig pointed out, we spend too much of our time asking, "What's new?" and not enough asking, "What's good?"

Perhaps it's best to think of this show as less of a concert and more of a Zen koan:

A fan asked Trey, "What is the true Phish nature?"

Trey pointed back to the fan and said, "You should show me the way of Phish."

The fan struggled to perform a song with no instruments. Confused, he exclaimed, "That pointless task did not further my understanding."

It was then that a traveling Fishman walked by. "It was the novelty of that creation that delighted me!" Jon cried. And in that moment, the fan was enlightened.

9: MAY 22, 1994 – VOGUE THEATRE
VANCOUVER, BC

Make a run to the border.

Thus enlightened, I left the ashram that was Seattle and headed north, past the tulip fields of Mt. Vernon, avoided the temptations of Chuckanut Drive[20] and North Cascades National Park, and went to the main border crossing at Blaine. One of the things that has changed over the decades is how targeted hippies are by the police. While there were occasional bust fests as recently as 2009, it was much more common in the 90s. Leftover antagonism from Grateful Dead tours spilled over into Phish.

Mind you, by the end of the 80s, Deadheads were far from innocent bystanders. Most people on tour were absolutely wonderful, but there were those who lived so close to the edge that they couldn't do much more than try to survive. They'd steal and use people's lawns as bathrooms and otherwise annoy the general community. For that matter, even the respected members of the community had little problem with spare changing or selling alcohol to minors or LSD to anyone. As frustrating as we must have been to local communities, it still felt like there regularly was too much man power devoted to stopping people who just wanted to see their concerts, celebrate life, and then move on to the next town. They put inspection checkpoints on tollbooths on I-95, hired undercovers to work the lot, and made a point of not wanting people to actually grab a nap in their rest stops. It would be much better for tired people to drive than to allow that!

Phish still was under the radar for the most part, but myself, not so much. I

---

[20] Chuckanut Drive is the back way from Mt. Vernon to Bellingham. There's a stunning 10 mile stretch that hugs Samish Bay. If you're ever driving from Seattle to Vancouver B.C., and have a few minutes to kill, getting off of I-5 and taking that detour is highly recommended. It's not that much of a long cut and if you follow it back around, it drops you back off at the highway.

had plenty of Phish and Dead stickers on my car and usually let my beard grow quite long. I figured I could get away with that for one obvious reason: I go to shows sober. I know for many people chemicals enhance a musical experience, making the concert even more intense, but I'm not wired that way. Of these 27 shows written about in this book, I would be cold sober at every one. The closest thing to chemical enhancement was the nightly Dr. Pepper to keep me awake. The music was always powerful enough on its own.

However, just because I know that I'm sober every night, doesn't mean that a Customs Agent would think the same if a ragged looking, young bearded male pulls up to their crossing in a Geo Metro plastered with Grateful Dead stickers and New Mexico plates. Not helping my cause was that I had left my bags (such as they were. I was traveling light.) back in Seattle. Crossing a border with non-local plates and little luggage raises all of the alarms. It looked like my streak of being pulled over and having the car searched would continue. Then though, they asked the fatal question. "What do you do for a living?" I answered honestly that I was a graduate student studying mathematics and teaching undergrads at New Mexico State.

Zzyzx Tour Lesson Number Five: *If authorities are harassing you because you conform to a particular stereotype in their mind, give them a different one to focus on. Bearded hippie guy is someone to search. Bearded math professor is a completely different image, one that has some vague prestige or at least presents a lack of concern in the pre-Unabomber days.*

Right before this long tour started, Phish released a new album. *Hoist* was somewhat controversial as it was a move away from Phish's progressive influence and more towards a hook based direction. One must keep that controversy in perspective, seeing how Phish fans are always accusing the band of selling out. Mike told a story in the Schvice about a fan who lamented the move from Nectar's to The Front. She was crying outside the venue, because, "They're not our band anymore." Mind you The Front still only holds 400 people, but that's the irony of Phish fans. We live for improvisation and change but then freak out when anything outside of our range of expectation happens.

The most interesting song on *Hoist* , the one that even the 1994 jaded people liked was the final song on the album, "Demand." The studio version of the song is kind of bizarre. The lyrics are fairly dark, a warning to prepare for the potential for disaster. It ends on a hopeful note, as the character is heading home for a relaxing weekend with his parents. There then is the sound effect of someone getting into a car and starting it up. He then pops in a tape – and, yes, it is amusing in the days of MP3s to hear the sound of someone inserting a cassette into a car deck – of the "Split Open and Melt" from 4/21/93. It's a pretty intense version, so it's not surprising that the driver starts driving faster and faster. First you can hear police sirens in the background, then the sound of his tires squealing as he's taking turns way too fast, and then – as the song ends – he crashes into a wall. There's then a quick a Capella section of "Yerushalayim Shel Zahav," to mourn his death.

It's a weird idea to kill a fan on your album, but without the studio tricks, "Demand" doesn't quite work too well. At least that seemed to be the conclusion as it was played three times early on this tour and then dropped. Perhaps they found it too Demanding. The advantage of playing outside of your hardcore fan region – and in this case even outside of their home country – is that you can experiment a little. Maybe you can salvage a song that wasn't clicking. I don't know if that was the reasoning, but phase two of seeing if "Demand" could stick in rotation happened in the Pacific Province[21].

Instead of segueing into "Split Open and Melt" (and traffic fatalities), the end of the lyric section immediately went into a quasi-rare song, "The Sloth." So much of the Phish experience is defined by our own personal shows. This would be the only time in 1994 I caught this ode to the only man in Gamehendge who could eliminate a king, so I think of it as extremely rare for this era. Meanwhile I saw "Harpua" three times in 1994, so that feels relatively common. Phish played "The Sloth" more often than "Harpua" this year, but my impressions are more important than mere facts. The opening

---

[21] For those wondering, it didn't. "Demand" was played 5 more times in summer 94, 4 in fall 95, once in fall 96, and one last time (to date) on 12/31/09.

combination stands out to me as pairing rarities.

One thing that's interesting about following Phish over a course of decades is that song patterns are discovered, explored for a while, and then abandoned. Early in Phish's career, "Wilson" was almost always followed by the Frank Zappa instrumental "Peaches en Regalia." "Runaway Jim" was paired with "Foam" enough to give fans an excuse to complain, but they weren't joined anytime after 7/19/96 until 2009 when the combination made a stunning comeback. Summer 1994 had a pairing unique to the era.

There was a streak where eight straight "Tweezers" (and nine out of ten; only the Bomb Factory insanity broke the pattern) were followed by *Hoist's* "Lifeboy." The combination does work well. Resolving the chaos – or, as in the case of this Vancouver version, straight forward rock and roll - into a ballad, switching from the nonsensical words of "Tweezer" to a song about atheism, or at least doubt, is the core of what the Phish experience can be all about.

Phish is a dichotomy. Jams and songs, silliness and darkness, chaos and form, at their best they can switch back and forth between these modes and keep changing up the sound. "Lifeboy" didn't stick around in this role – these days it's put in the never ever played slot – but it worked very well for the summer.

As annoying as Canadian customs can be, the real hassles always seem to occur coming back into the States. This night was no exception. I wasn't just asked questions, but I got pulled over into the extra inspection line, the one where you have to pull over and get out of your car while they rip it apart looking for whatever they can find. Being stopped there was a rite of passage for me but this time had something that stuck in my memory.

While the agents were searching my car and finding out that I was indeed boring, I was waiting inside the customs' building. The woman behind the counter had my driver's license hostage to make sure that I couldn't go anywhere. She looked at it, and said, "'David Steinberg?' Are you Jewish?"

One thing to understand about the generation of Jews that lived through World War II is that they became defined by the era with both paranoia and a sense of survival. They used that to infect their descendants. Sometimes it was cute – as in my grandmother's need to sing "God Bless America" at the end of every Seder or her rule that we could not have Japanese or German cars; my Aunt Francis once tried to convince her that BMW stood for "British Motor Works." – others (such as the long joke my grandfather told me one year that had the moral "They'll try to kill us, but we'll survive anyway!") a little on the disturbing side. The contagion worked though. When asked about my religious heritage by an agent of the US Government upon trying to reenter my country, I came close to panicking. Was a new law passed outlawing Jews with this being the first sign of its manifestation? Maybe I just had read *The Handmaid's Tale* one time too many, but there was a long dramatic pause as I tried to figure out the many, many reasons why she would be asking this question and how much trouble I was in, before it finally occurred to me that she was just making small talk. I wonder if she had any idea about the fear she created.

10: MAY 23, 1994 – CIVIC AUDITORIUM PORTLAND, OR

In which a major metropolitan region lets me know this would not be my home.

In many ways Portland, OR is much more my style than Seattle. Seattle has endless sprawl to the north and south – Puget Sound and the Cascades restrict the west and east expansion – which is exceedingly annoying to deal with. Portland drops off into woods and small towns much quicker. Two of my favorite venues in the northwest – Horning's Hideout and The Crystal Ballroom - are located there. I'm a fan of the non-corporate approach (although the flip of that – the job market – is an obvious Seattle advantage). There's a reason why the show is named *Portlandia* and not *Seattleia*.

So why didn't I end up in the Rose City? A large amount of that has to do with the welcomes the cities gave me. As mentioned above, my first day in Seattle featured stunning weather and incredible amounts of energy. Portland, not so much. It was one of those typical late spring Pacific Northwest days, the type that caused people to invent the phrase, "June Gloom." The highs were in the upper 50s – maybe even the low 60s - and it wasn't raining, but the sky was that deep grey that seems to hang out for months on end. The fog seems to suck out every ounce of heat from the air, like a Dementor.[22] As for the venue, the outside resembled a courthouse. There was little around the venue – at least not in 1994 – so one was left to sit outside on a chilly day looking at a nondescript building. It wasn't the warmest welcome in both literal and figurative senses.

What easily could have saved the night would have been some sort of epic concert, something to remember the event and infuse the name "Civic

---

[22] A monster in the Harry Potter universe. They suck all of the joy and happiness from the world, leaving behind only a mist and a sensation of intense cold. It's not too surprising that these books were written in a climate similar to the Northwest's.

Auditorium" with warm and fuzzy memories. That unfortunately is not what occurred. Part of that is not the show's fault. It's a solid enough show. The "Maze" and "Reba" are fiery. While "Run Like An Antelope" largely stays in the structure of the song – well until the end of the version when the "Rye Rye Rocco" section is all delivered in a creepy whisper. Trey murmurs the lines a few times with additional creepy asides. "Pretty senorita," and "I kill you!" were mixed in with the normal lyrics - it is a great reminder of just how powerful this song is. Continuing the theme of disturbing personalities, the "You Enjoy Myself," contains a verse and chorus of "Psycho Killer."

That's what this show was. It was a solid night with a standout "Run Like an Antelope." That's not much different than the Bee Cave show, but when I think of The Backyard, I immediately run to say that it has an underrated "Run Like an Antelope" that gets overshadowed by the previous night. When I think of this Portland show – to the degree that I ever do – it solely is to remember the "Psycho Killer" tease. This is despite the fact that the Portland "Antelope" might very well be the better one of the two and no one ever even thinks about considering to ponder the idea of mentioning this performance as something special.

Why do I remember one and not the other? Some of that is set and setting – the Backyard and the adventure getting there was more interesting – but largely it has to do with its placement on the tour for me.

When you hit the road and go on tour, at first there's a lot of excitement. Road trip!!! I get to see Phish tonight! I wonder what they'll play! After a few days though, it becomes less of an adventure, and more just what you do. Seeing too many shows in a row causes you to bitch about perfectly good songs just because it feels redundant. When your plans are flexible - it was easy to hop on and off of tour at will in the 90s since tickets didn't have to be purchased in advance most nights and they stuck around the same region for multiple shows – it's always good to know when it's time to take a break.

Zzyzx Tour Lesson Number Six: *If your reaction to most songs starting up is annoyance instead of delight, if you're only going because you're praying for a bustout or* *because you're terrified that you'll miss THE show, then it's probably time to take a break for a few nights. It's always best to remember that this is supposed to be fun, not an ordeal.*

However, as logical as that rule is, I was committed. The road back home – especially with a free place to stay in San Francisco – led through the Warfield. Three more shows on this leg for me. I pulled into the magical three level rest stop just south of town, one that gets you so far away from Interstate 5 that you can't even hear the road noise,[23] and went to sleep. Come the morning it would be time to follow the lines going south.

---

[23] This is my favorite rest stop I have ever slept in. You pull so far away from the Interstate that it feels more like a campground. As for the worst rest stops, those would be the ones in Ohio. During my years of rest stop camping, they had a state law that said you had to sign a form – along with your license plate and the current time – if you wanted to sleep in your car. Many states had very short allowable parking times, but only Ohio set up a means to enforce those.

For the record, while there are frequent horror stories presented about the dangers of using a highway exit as a free campground, I personally was lucky enough to never have encountered too much sketchiness. Perhaps the weirdest event was coming home from The Backyard. While taking a quick break along US 290, I saw some graffiti in the bathroom. The message had the current date and said that if anyone wanted to have relationships with his wife, he would be parked towards the back of the area. I took that as a cue to get back in my car.

11: MAY 25-27, 1994 – WARFIELD THEATRE
SAN FRANCISCO, CA

My faith is restored via branded macaroni and cheese.

One advantage to the timing of this tour is that my undergraduate years were not far behind. We all graduated and spread across the country but we still were writing letters to each other. In an era before the time where credit cards were handed out to college students in orientation, it was always a challenge to figure out where to stay, especially when one's budget was largely how much profit they made selling sodas for a dollar in the parking lot post show minus expenses for ticket cost, food [24], and gas. Being able to crash on friends' couches was always a crucial component to the tour budget. In San Francisco, I was lucky enough to be able to stay with Seth.

While the download era changes this dramatically, students – especially male students – in the late 1980s were able to create an identity out of media possession. Take tape trading for example. For lovers of live music, it came down to tape collections. You had to find your fellow Deadheads/Phish fans/Spreadnecks/etc. and cultivate relations with them. You couldn't just latch onto one and copy their entire library – although most people were pretty generous with theirs and loved to share the jewels of their collection – but had to find multiple sources. Ideally you would be able to find seven or eight good collections and cull out the best that they had. Then you use those tapes to try to find others outside of your region; "My list gets yours," was a

---

[24] Tour diet in summer 94 was a lot of fruit, bread, and canned food. I didn't have a credit card and my job in New Mexico paid all of $720 a month, so it's not like it is now where tour is partially an excuse for me to explore new restaurants in exciting towns. Fortunately many of these venues were in areas where you could get a slice of pizza for a dollar or two. With all of the walking around, the dancing, and the inability to afford much food, I always lost weight on tour. Maybe I could call this *The Tour Diet* and promote this book in the self-help section!

common sign off in tape trading ads in the back of Relix. Ideally you would then be able to get goodies that none of your original traders had and you could then return the favor.

It sounds nice and utopian, but let's be honest, we all knew that there was an element of judging involved. You always wanted to be the person with the lower generation seed (important because cassette tapes lost fidelity with each additional copy made from the master), the best taping equipment – two decks were needed to be able to set levels properly, no dual decks, and definitely no high speed dubbing unless you wanted Jerry to sound like Mickey Mouse after a few generations – and the perfect blanks.

Tapes came in various qualities. Due to incredible marketing, Maxell rapidly became the brand of choice for the tape trading community, even though some swore that the equivalent TDKs sounded better and had less tape hiss. Better quality tapes allowed you to increase the levels – how loud the music was on the tape – without introducing distortion. This let you reduce the dreaded hiss and was the key to getting almost pristine copies. Better tapes were also less prone to breaking and falling apart upon repeated plays.

In the early days of my collecting period, I got lucky. I met someone off campus who agreed to spin me a few tapes. This was right around the time that the Betty Boards dropped. Betty Cantor-Jackson was a sound engineer for the Grateful Dead who recorded the shows on her own machine when she was working. These recordings were stored in a storage unit until she was unable to make the rent on them. A fan bid for them, made copies and started circulating them. These tapes were far above anything – both in terms of sound quality and the playing at the show – that were circulating. My five tapes I received were all low generation Betty Boards, including the infamous May 8, 1977 Cornell show. I was the first person at Bard who had these, and was easily able to parley them into the core of a great collection.

While Seth was one of the people with whom I traded tapes, that was far from his only media interest. He had a wall of records along a wall of his dorm room. The best way to learn about new music then - unless you were lucky enough to have an amazing radio station – was to have a friend like Seth. He subscribed to music magazines, read reviews, and bought albums.

The indie DIY movement was just starting. The music was there but being able to find out about it was less easy. The Velvet Underground, The Young Fresh Fellows, The Long Ryders, the insane Beatles cover band Tater Totz – alas their amazing album *Alien Sleestacks from Brazil* is impossible to find on the Internet. Apparently a studio fire destroyed the master tapes before they made CDs of the release – so many bands I grew to love, I first heard in his dorm room. In fact, I owe my Phish career to him.

Another way that people used to discover bands was through random happenstance. After my admissions interview at Bard in 1987, I wanted to see what a college bookstore was all about. Unlike major universities that largely sell shirts and sweats for fans of their athletic programs, Bard's focused on selling ink on pulped wood. The campus is close enough to New York City that they sold *The Village Voice*. That seemed rather exotic to an 18 year old Baltimorean. I bought and devoured it.

This issue reviewed the Camper Van Beethoven album *Telephone Free Landslide Victory*. Upon returning home, I purchased it largely because I loved the name of the band. The album is a bizarre amalgamation of ska and punk. Its humorous lyrics disguise that there's a philosophy underneath, a frustration over the uselessness of any sort of action. It was the perfect soundtrack for the late Reagan years. I fell in love with the band in the way that only teenagers first developing their own tastes can do.

Two years later, now at Bard instead of thinking about attending there, a crisis was brewing. Bard had a traditional Halloween party that waxed Dionysian. The school has a hippie image – it is just across the Hudson from Woodstock, there was a famous drug bust there in the 60s, its most famous attendees are Chevy Chase and the founding members of Steely Dan, Dylan used to hang out there and referenced a pump on campus in "Subterranean Homesick Blues" - that they were fighting with, unsure if they should embrace it or dive completely into the Just Say No world of the 80s. In an attempt to clean things up, a woman named Beth Frumpkin was brought in and given the unfortunate title of Dean of Drug and Alcohol Abuse. The Halloween party might be no more.

While people were fretting over this, a Vermonter named Jasmine gave

Seth a copy of *Junta* to review for *The Bard Observer*. They were on the eve of their first Poughkeepsie show which he presented as a Halloween alternative. He was not particularly subtle about this. After saying that the sight of Phish playing on trampolines might induce trails, he concluded, "I think the Chance show will be the best choice for a hippy (rhymes with) Halloween." Partially in an attempt to get me to go to the show, he described them in the article as sounding "like Camper Van Beethoven covering Steely Dan or Steely Dan covering early Pink Floyd." The effort worked.

I went to the show with no expectations. In fact I attended largely because a Bard band named Shooky Bones was opening. "This Phish band should be opening for you," I said to the guitarist. He disagreed and told me to check out their sets.

I don't remember much about this show, and alas no one – not even the band – recorded it, but based on my memories and a review in *The Observer* I am able to piece together some details. Mainly, there were two different story songs in the second set. "Colonel Forbin's Ascent" largely just confounded me. It seemed to be just another song until Trey said, "Now some of you might be confused about what's going on here...." and then told the Gamehendge story. Actually Trey I just thought it was a song, but now that you're telling a story and your voice is muddled in the mix, I'm lost.

Fortunately they fixed the acoustics for the second set closing "Harpua." Yes, I saw "Harpua" at my first show; it would take exactly three years and one month until I saw my second one. This is where I first got the band. It was an inspired version. The story – a little tale about a suburban battle to the death between feline and canine – had two twists that stuck with me. One was the long build up to revealing the name of Jimmy's cat. "Your name. The name I gave you. I loved you so much that when I first saw you, I just had to call you by this name. The name... It's not 'Fluff.'" This went on for quite some time before the reveal of the moniker Poster Nutbag. Later Trey described that Poster jumped onto the "white... corduroy... shelf." The story revealed a surrealist sense of humor that I always have been partial to.

I went to the merchandise table post show and looked at the the cassettes of *Junta*. One of the songs on it was called "Fluffhead." I remembered Trey's

"It's not 'Fluff!'" and bought the album, hoping that that was the name of the song. It wasn't of course, but the album did contain "Divided Sky." I was floored by the beauty of the composition and saw them again a few weeks later at Pearl Street... and then again on 12/30 and 12/31/89 on their first New Years' Run.

My Phish love came down to *Junta*, I bought the album because I attended that particular show – without the random line that I've never heard in any other "Harpua," it's quite possible that I don't actually purchase the album and might not have gone to a second show for years later - and I attended that show because of Seth and his appeal to my Camper Van Beethoven fascination.

Post-Bard, he lived in the Haight. While I had been to San Francisco before, I didn't know what to expect from the neighborhood we all romanticized. At the time it was in flux, part tourist trap for hippies (what it is now) but also had an actual grungy element from what few down and outers still lived there. A lot of San Francisco was like that then. Walking to the Warfield, amused at seeing that Fillmore was actually a road name, it struck me how the neighborhoods mixed. A wealthy area would be adjacent to a housing project and no one seemed to care. The tech gentrification had yet to happen – Bob Weir sang in the late 80s Grateful Dead song "Picasso Moon" about "South of Market in the land of ruin." Nowadays if you go south of Market Street, you're largely in the land of Google, leading to some interesting contrasts. It was fascinating to observe but I made sure to take the bus back.

When staying in the Haight and thinking about other San Francisco icons and how they affected the early Grateful Dead years, it would only be appropriate to see Phish at The Warfield. The converted vaudeville theatre was home to the legendary fifteen show run in 1980. Every night started out with an acoustic set, a rarity for the Grateful Dead world outside of this and the sister run at Radio City Music Hall. Jerry loved to play here; there were nearly 100 solo Garcia shows at The Warfield. For a Deadhead turned Phish fan, this was an incredibly exciting moment. [25]

---

[25] Five years later I would return to The Warfield to see the first ever combination project of members of Phish and the Dead. Featuring bassist Phil Lesh (and a

A curtain was draped across the stage before the first show, akin to what you would see before a play started. The lights went out and as the curtain was raised, Phish engaged in a little musical pun, starting the song with that title.

"The Curtain" is one of Phish's first songs. It was debuted back in 1987, deep in the proto-history of Phish. There are two things to know about this song. The first is that there's no obvious reason whatsoever why this song is called "The Curtain." The few lyrics do not have any references to draperies of any sort. They're haunting but enigmatic, starting with, "As he saw his life run away from him, thousands ran along chanting words from a song." Does this mean that this is curtains for the singer? Does all of this happen behind some sort of curtain? Did it just sound good to someone in the band when they were looking for a title? We will never know.

What is known about "The Curtain" is that this song has two arrangements. "The Curtain With" is the more complicated version. It has a long, composed arrangement at the end, one that is quite stunning but also hard to play. The "With" section was abandoned for over a decade after 1988[26], but it still lived on. A section of it was stolen and became the second arrangement for the song "Rift."

Part of the fun of listening to the early days of Phish is that so little of what we know about these songs is true. Songs debuted before 1990 – even a little later if you include the lyric changes to "Runaway Jim," "The Horse," and "Bouncing Around the Room" along with the two versions of "Rift" – are subject to change. The long composition of "Fluffhead" was once a collection of stand alone songs. Most of "Divided Sky" existed inside a song named "No Dogs Allowed" for a while. "Tela" changed every other time it was played with new bridges and ending vocal sections added before the band

---

surprise appearance by the Dead's 1970's backup singer Donna Jean Godchaux) and Trey and Page from Phish, the setlists mostly came from the Grateful Dead world with a few Phish songs mixed in. Even after Jerry had passed, The Warfield still had this connection.

[26] It was returned to rotation in Deer Creek in 2000 after a gap of over 1000 shows, one of the 5 longest gaps in Phish's history. Few people collect recording before 1993 or so, so a lot of people were quite confused and just wrote "slow 'Rift' jam?!" in their setlists.

realized that they didn't really work. The middle part of "Punch You in the Eye" was ripped out and became "The Landlady." After a few years "PYITE" was brought back and "The Landlady" collected her rents for Wilson.

If you love Phish – really love Phish – but don't listen to recordings before 1994, it's actually worth your time to check these out. It's not the same music that you know, but it gives a cool insight into how these songs evolved. It's easy to see worlds where "You Enjoy Myself" is a minute long vocal jam section (like it is in the demo version on *The White Tape*), and this band never quite makes it out of clubs. One of the great things about Phish is that all of the missteps and random directions they tried are available for us to explore. How did Phish get big? They experimented relentlessly and had no problem abandoning or changing songs if they decided the version that they've already played didn't work.

Another reason for their success is that they were willing to be true to themselves and just hope that fans liked it. When you have fans following you around the country, that creates a dilemma: some people only are going to see their local show and want to see their favorite songs but others are on their 12th show of the run and are sick of the songs in rotation. How do you balance those issues? Phish's plan always leaned towards not thinking about it too much. If they played what they wanted, the audience would hopefully follow. With a fanbase as fractured as Phish's is – they have one of the few groups where the phrase "crowd pleasing song" usually gets used as an insult– there's always a group that's excited by the long jams and another that wishes they'd end the noodling and find a song to play. With a few exceptions (such as sets at multiband festivals which normally would focus on the songs instead of extended jams) Phish do what they feel. Sometimes that's a long jam, sometimes it's jumping to the next song, and sometimes it's choosing for their opener based on an obscure joke that only a few people in attendance would get.

There's a little parlor game with Phish fans. We love discovering teases of other songs buried within Phish jams. Sometimes it's obviously just a coincidence, caused by there being only so many tasteful arrangements of notes. There might be a few seconds in the 12/31/95 "Drowned" that sound a bit like the Grateful Dead's "Fire on the Mountain" if you stand on your head and squint and there's a little jam in the 9/3/11 "Piper" that so wants to be the Modern Lovers' "Roadrunner," complete with a singing of something that isn't "Radio on," but almost is to a melody that is almost the melody of that song but isn't. Diehards will argue back and forth about it, causing setlists to be constantly rewritten with the current consensus over whether that is a tease or not. When people get lost in these debates – and they can get surprisingly argumentative for something this pointless – there's usually someone who mentions that it's annoying that we feel the need to label every thing that sounds vaguely like another song. In defense of those who play this game, let me present Exhibit A: the 5/25/94 "Stash."

Following "The Curtain" and "Sample in a Jar," Phish covered the Bill Monroe song "Uncle Pen." The lyrics of the song mention a band that plays two other bluegrass songs, the classics "Soldier's Joy," and "Boston Boy." Phish's arrangement of "Uncle Pen" has an instrumental section where those two songs are played. The "Stash" that followed has a section in the jam where Trey plays the instrumental part they added to "Uncle Pen." Let's be precise. During "Stash" Trey teases a part in their arrangement of "Uncle Pen" that teases a traditional bluegrass song "Boston Boy." If they're going to play that kind of game, I can promise you that people are going to be paying attention to every note played in hopes that Mike will accidentally stumble across a Mumford and Sons song. In the words of 3rd graders everywhere: They started it!

While the first night had a few things to make it stick in my mind – in addition to the above, there was an always fun "Colonel Forbin's Ascent." Trey tells a story in that song, usually about how we all end up transported to Gamehendge. In this case it was a giant slingshot that sent us there – the second is a blank slate. This is the nature of tour. If they all were the best show ever, then that would just become a routine and we'd start to get jaded over even those.

Proof of that comes from the following night. May 26, 1994 is a show that no one ever talks about. It has zero reviews on Phish.net. Despite that, it has versions of songs that would be legendary (or at least in best of the year conversation) in any other period. Take the "Demand" > "Split Open and Melt" for example. Paired together as they were on *Hoist*, the end of the

"Melt" becomes music to speed to. As the jam gets louder and faster, Trey starts screaming at the peaks, a sort of vocal callback to the squealing tires on the album. Play that in 2010 and people would rave as long there were electrons willing to be sacrificed to send messages on the Internet. The "It's Ice," "Divided Sky," "Run Like An Antelope," and "Fluffhead," were also all well above average versions, performances that would get people fired up, were it not that there were other shows in the immediate proximity that had slighter better ones. Then again, this is a gym show, one you listen to while on the treadmill and find yourself moving quite quickly, and those are always underrated.

The third night of the Warfield would be my 12th since the Bomb Factory concert that started my year. After this night I would be heading back home with a decision to make. A lot was riding on this concert.

The Friday night show opened with "Wilson." When I say that, this puts an image in the mind of Phish fans. Trey plays the opening "Ba-bump, Ba-bump" riff and thousands of people chant "Wilson." Originally the Wilson chant was performed by Trey. In late 1992 continuing into early 1993, the introductions became longer and more interesting, with extra fills and brief spacey interludes played between the bombastic theme, until the evil king's name was finally chanted a few token times. As late as the 1993 New Years' Run, the appellation was vocalized by everyone's favorite redheaded guitarist. When did that change?

It looks like the switchover was a mere month before the Bomb Factory. April 9, 1994 in Binghamton had the delayed chant. The next time "Wilson" was performed was six days later in Manhattan's Beacon Theatre. The northeast, even more so in in the early 90s than today, was the center of the Phish fan universe and New Yorkers are not exactly known for their patience. After a few passes the crowd – perhaps inspired by an enthusiastic Brent Alohab[27] - got restless. They knew what was supposed to happen there. If Trey wasn't going to announce the king, they would take that task upon themselves.

---

[27]At least according to Scott Bernstein's remembrance of his first Phish show posted on http://www.glidemagazine.com/hiddentrack/14-years-ago-phish-the-beacon/

While it's true that once fans start doing something in the Phish world, it's very hard for it ever to stop, it took longer for the word to get out. It took multiple repetitions for the chant to first start and then get pretty loud. The idea was still in its infancy – it would later take off at their first Madison Square Garden concert that winter and the subsequent release of that performance on *Live Phish* – but it didn't quite catch on yet. It's a shame to have lost the intriguing variations on the introduction that were starting to happen, but sometimes those die off anyway. It's worth it for that moment when 20,000 people join forces. Names have power; chanting "Wilson" will prevent the king from doing his dire deed![28]

Unlike the books of cliché, "David Bowies" frequently can be judged by their intros. The song starts with Fishman playing a pattern on the cymbal. Sometimes that leads right into the start of the main section of the song, but others take a different direction. The other three members play interesting patterns on top of the rhythm. A good rule of thumb is that any attempt to stretch it out a bit usually bodes well. If it gets so interesting that Fishman moves to the main drum kit, that's an even more auspicious portent. This version had a brief introductory section, but it was surprisingly interesting for only being 50 seconds long. The jam took a similar pattern. It mostly stuck to the standard formula for the song, starting quiet and slow, slowly building until it hit the peak of Trey's ridiculously fast circular riff at the end, but still finding a way of carving out a unique sound.

Phish love to play games with tension and release. The end of "Fluffhead" has a riff repeated over and over again (sometimes with the lyrics, "La la la la la/Life is just a bundle of joy," sung over it, frequently in a menacing manner)

---

[28] As a Seahawks fan, I must also mention the lasting effect of this chant. Early in 2013 Trey decided to link the chant to quarterback Russell Wilson, saying that if we chanted it for him at Seahawks' Stadium, there would be a guaranteed Super Bowl. Somehow it caught on. The stadium started chanting it. The downtown Ferris Wheel made a video with the song. The mayor of Seattle started tweeting links to the song to the cities Seattle was playing. There was an NFL Films Production that had Trey in it.

It culminated in the Seahawks winning their first Super Bowl and Russell Wilson walking into the celebration at the stadium, holding up the Lombardi Trophy as "Wilson" played over the PA. It was an incredible mix of two of my obsessions.

until it finally explodes into the bliss that is "Arrival." The peak of "David Bowie" uses a similar technique in general.

May 27 had a double example of exhilaration through tension's liberation. As the jam starts to build, there's a detour to a repetition on a rather creepy pattern. Each pass makes it slightly darker, slightly eerier. There's an attempt to end the weirdness but it immediately returns to darkness, only faster this time. Fast jams are normally like driving down a highway at 80 mph. Instead of doing so on a sunny day for the joy of it, this time you're on a 2 lane dirt road… at night… in a driving rainstorm… while being chased by monsters. They're getting closer and closer, you get more and more panicked, and then suddenly, it changes to euphoric! Tension and relief, making the amazing peak stand out that much more due to the eeriness preceding it. When done well – and this version is indeed done well – it's hard to resist.

One advantage of playing theatres is that there are incredible acoustics. Starting with the barbershop quartet songs and then expanding to acoustic arrangements of other songs, they tried performing songs with no amplification. The experiment was always a bit of a mixed success. There's no way of keeping a 1500 person crowd completely quiet. Some fans would try to shush the others but all that did was add to the noise. Inevitably someone would scream something when we all quieted down and then that would lead to a loud cheer. It was even worse as a taper. You had to crank the levels as up as high as they would go to even have a chance of hearing any of it, which led to desperation level lowering when the song ended and crowd roared. More than any other number Phish did, the quiet songs were of the moment.

At least that's true normally. On this night it was my past and my present precisely divided. Phish was joined in the no amplification club by violinist Morgan Fichter of Camper Van Beethoven. She sat in on "Nellie Kane" and "My Mind's Got a Mind of its Own." While it's hard to hear her contribution on the recordings, this guest appearance felt like a personal message. On a night when I was staying with Seth, Phish played with a member of the band he used to inspire me to take a Chance.

Returning to les instruments électriques, Phish fired up "Mike's Song." The jam in this didn't last long before Trey started singing, "We've got it simple, 'cause we've got a band." This would be the first of the five proto-"Simples" of summer 94. This version has speed going for it. It's much faster than the song it would become. The standard riff that most people think of as being "Simple" was barely played at all. Instead variants of the lyrics were sung over music that was more akin to a "Mike's Song" jam than an actual song.

Phish have a song titled "Catapult," that is basically an anti-song. It has a standard small set of lyrics but they can be sung over pretty much any tune – sometimes it's even chanted - and the music can be whatever the band is feeling at the moment. The only thing that makes it Catapult is that those particular words are said/sung/whispered/yodeled. At this point in its development "Simple" was even less of a song than that. Not only did the music morph, but the lyrics were whatever variant of "Cymbop and Beebaphone" sounded good in the moment.

"Mike's Song" picked back up when "Simple" ended. It quickly fell into a beautiful jam, something that was very impressive to be a spontaneous creation. There's a reason for that. It actually was a Puccini aria "O Mio Babbino Caro." The reason why we all know that is that the jam stopped and opera singer Andrea Baker emerged to sing. For the second time that night there would be a guest and for the second time she would perform with no amplification.

Trey wasn't slacking while Baker sang. He had a task. Boxes of Kraft Flintstone's Macaroni and Cheese were handed out to the crowd. Throughout the "Possum" that followed, we were instructed to "Shake your macaroni!" There was a third unamplified guest, and that would be us.

What is the sound of 1000 boxes of macaroni and cheese shaking? If you're in the middle of it, it sounds rather percussive and impressive. Sure, after the fact it sounds more like static or tape hiss than anything else, but it was amazing to be there, playing a DYI percussion instrument. When I'm on my deathbed, in the final moments before the houselights are turned up on my life, I'm sure to devote one or two them on the night where we got to "Shake shake shake, through the drum break."

We were supposed to donate the boxes to a food bank, but I just couldn't do so. I later gave a New Mexico agency the price of a box of macaroni and cheese; this one I kept. It's the oldest food I have, even though now I'd be terrified to open it; the only thing more horrifying than it looking disgusting would be if it had so many chemicals that it was still well preserved.

Phish would have two more shows on this leg, playing at the Laguna Seca Daze Festival but it was time for me to go home for a few weeks. It's a full day drive from the Bay Area to Las Cruces. The most direct route passes near Las Vegas and that inspired a long cut.

One of the most frequent questions I receive is people wondering where "Zzyzx" came from. When I was in high school, I went on a teen tour. We rode around in a bus and saw the vast majority of the country. Of course when you go to a different city and a different tourist attraction every single day, it all merges together into some bizarre melding of t-shirts and bad photos and long bus rides. What stands out is not seeing Old Faithful or the Grand Canyon, but the spaces between the attractions. One was along I-15 between Los Angeles and Vegas. I'm no longer sure what exactly they had in mind for 16 year olds to do in Vegas in the mid 80s, but I still remembered looking out on the side of the highway and seeing an exit for "Zzyzx Road." The name was so bizarre that it stuck with me. I started to use it as a faux pseudonym. These can morph rather quickly into real ones once you're on the Internet, so Zzyzx it would be.

I was close enough to Baker, CA that I had to route myself in that direction. I figured I would get out there and maybe something fascinating would happen. The only concern I had was that maybe there would be a cop there who would wonder what I was doing, but what would be the odds of that. Still though, I couldn't shake that feeling so – for some reason – I parked on the exit ramp and walked to Zzyzx Road. Sitting on the road, completely blocking it, were two police cars. I looked at them, puzzled, and just walked back to my car.

I have since been back to explore the region and have seen just how isolated it is. I have no idea why it would be considered a good use of police resources to stop curious motorists from seeing what Zzyzx Road is (especially because it's just a dirt road that leads to a desert research center), nor do I know what gave me the feeling that they would be there. It's a bizarre moment all around; my enlightenment was prevented.

To make up for this disappointment, I stopped at a gas station just outside of Las Vegas. While I was waiting for my tank to fill, I put a quarter in a slot machine. I won fifty cents and quickly cashed out. This would be my only trip to Vegas between the Teen Tour (where I was underage and didn't gamble) and 1998's Halloween run. For the first 29 years of my life, I could honestly claim to be ahead of Vegas. Sure it was only by a quarter, but there aren't many who can say that. Take that billion dollar industry!

12: JUNE 10-11, 1994 – RED ROCKS AMPITHEATRE MORRISON, CO

Phish play the best show of their career and no one notices.

Once back in New Mexico, I had a choice. I could either go back to my new love that was the Pacific Northwest to see some Grateful Dead shows or stay in the Phish universe and head towards the Midwest. Optimize my music preference or go for my favorite region. Maybe if I didn't have the excuse of visiting my family if I kept heading east, perhaps if the Phoenix Grateful Dead shows from the previous March weren't so mediocre, possibly if macaroni hadn't just been shaken, I might have headed in the other direction. However I did, they were, and it was, so first I was to go north, and then east. Not once have I ever regretted that call. Usually a plan that starts out at Red Rocks is going to be a good one.

What makes Red Rocks so stunning is that it wasn't created by man. Sure, architects and construction crews were hired to put in the benches and make the stage, but the general structure of the venue, the acoustics and incredible view all existed eons before Trey wrote "You Enjoy Myself."

Phish had played in Morrison once before. The previous August saw Phish at their 1993 best. The always chaotic Colorado weather brought a present to the attendees in the form of a giant rainstorm. The venue was well prepared for such matters and had plastic ponchos for sale emblazoned with, "I was rained on at the Rocks." As happens so frequently in the Front Range in August, the storm rolled in, was insanely powerful, and then vanished. The rain stopped right at the 7:30 show time. The wind was still whipping through our ponchos but we were able to stay dry.

Phish opened up that night appropriately with "Divided Sky" (as the sky was still half covered with storm clouds), "Harpua" (for the "Look, the storm's gone," line). Trey's "Harpua," story digressed quite a bit from the usual title bout of canine v feline. This time it was about the history of Red Rocks. Harpua learned how to shape shift and turned himself into a giant iguana. Poster Nutbag had such a powerful stare that he turned the iguana to stone in the red rocky cliff.[29]

Between the giant iguana references, the intriguing early arrangement of "The Wedge," and Jon Fishman's mom Mimi coming out to play the vacuum, this show would have stood out, but there was one moment from 8/20/93 that I will never forget. One of my all time favorite Phish songs was – and still is to this day – "Slave to the Traffic Light." Unfortunately, right around the time of my first show, Phish decided they didn't like playing it. It came out a few times a year until 1991 when it was retired until early August 1993. Phish had a show at the zoo in Cincinnati. They were unable to resist singing, "See the city, see the zoo," in an actual zoo, so the song returned. It was played twice more in 1993, on 12/30 after a determined crowd chanted for it, and – yes – at Red Rocks.

Anyone who follows an improvisational band around knows that moment. There's a song that you've always wanted to hear. You keep missing it. After way too many shows, it's suddenly played. Regardless of the quality of the version, there's an uncontrollable euphoria. It might be odd that the choice of setlist selection can be so powerful, but I refuse to analyze the reasons behind it lest that cause it to disappear. Incredible happiness is better than pure understanding. Suffice it to say that when Phish played "Slave" on 8/20/93, I would have been beaming regardless. In this case it also was a very solid version and off in the distance I could see the storm striking over downtown Denver. There are moments on tour that are seared in our memories forever.

Moving back to the 1994 run, It would be nice to say that June 10 had some more of those, but even sans life changing songs, the Rocks can deliver. While some of the highlights are where you'd expect them to be – the "Tweezer," while not quite up there with the Bomb Factory, hits some very

---

[29] For decades I wondered what Trey was talking about. That finally changed during a day trip to Red Rocks during the Dick's run in 2013. When there's no show, you can walk on the stage. From that angle it was suddenly clear. You have to be standing there, but there is indeed a formation in the rocks that kind of looks like an iguana.

nice peaks in its fifteen minutes – two of them are more unusual. "The Lizards" had an introduction that first was reminiscent of "Leprechaun"[30] and then referenced the iguana from the year before. Even better was the Fishman vacuum section.

Phish has never been above goofy antics. One of the sillier ones is when Fishman comes out from behind his drum kit. His trip to the front of the stage is soundtracked by Argent's "Hold Your Head Up." This is due to the fact that he let the rest of the band know in no uncertain terms that he hates the song when they fell into it during a practice.[31] It's usually a Syd Barrett song that he performs, although Prince's "Purple Rain," Marvin Gaye's "Sexual Healing," and Pink Floyd's "Great Gig in the Sky," were also fair game. The Fishman section is somewhat controversial among fans. Some love the silliness while others think that it takes up valuable time that could be used for a jam. Like everything in the Phish world, as this has become more infrequent over the years, it's also become a lot more popular.

It's fun to hear silly little takes on great songs, but there's potential for more. That's proved by the cover played this night, *The Jungle Book's* "I Wanna Be Like You." Even with Fishman struggling with the lyrics, the groove of the song works very well for a bass/drums/piano trio. The background scat singing behind Fishman's vocals is infectious. Unfortunately, this would be the final of the nine versions Phish have played. If this song had stuck around, even those who hate the sillier aspects of Phish would be charmed.

Towards the tail end of this summer, I would be taping a show in Philadelphia. I didn't have my own microphones, so I would plug into another taper's deck. While waiting for the show to start I struck up a conversation with him. It turned out that he taped the Grateful Dead's famous 5/8/77 Cornell show. Due in part to the incredible sound quality of the Betty Board that circulated, but mainly because of the insanely good "Scarlet>Fire," "St. Stephen > Not Fade Away > St. Stephen" and a ridiculously powerful

---

[30] "Leprechaun was a beautiful little instrumental song that was played three times, all in July 1993. It appeared a few times later in soundchecks, but has long since been abandoned. It sounds a little like a Penguin Café Orchestra song.

[31] There were stretches where "Cold as Ice" and the Cars' "Let's Go" took the place of "Hold Your Head Up." It's safe to assume that Jon hates those songs too.

"Morning Dew," this show is widely considered to be one of the best that the Dead have ever played. I asked him what the experience was like being at a legendary show, but that wasn't the reaction at the time. People liked the show well enough, but it was considered to be another great show in a run of excellent concerts.

Every live music fan knows the experience of coming home from an amazing concert, getting a recording of it, and finding out that it just doesn't hold up. That's the more common experience, but sometimes the flip is true. A show can come to define an era years later. There are reasons why this happens. If a show is the only one in a period that has a soundboard, if the highlights are more the about the quality of what is played instead of the novelty of the song selection, if there are aspects of the show that were common to the era but less so in later ones, if it's more a series of well above average songs instead of one or two epic versions with filler, all of these can lead toward a concert becoming highly regarded well after the fact. June 11, 1994 is one of those concerts.

The odd thing about Phish's fanbase is that it isn't one. Instead it's a couple disparate groups welded together. In most fandoms there's some sense of agreement as to what the band's best songs are, or at least what style of music is to be wished for. Phish appeal on a few different levels. This has created the odd situation of multiple interest groups existing. We all agree that we love to see Phish, but some people live for banter and stories whereas others consider that to be a waste of valuable set real estate. There are prog rock fans who focus on the complex compositions of the *Junta* and *Lawn Boy* era and dance partiers who want "Punch You in the Eye" played every night. Set list geeks look for bustouts; in the day of the Internet, you can find people Tweeting about the most trivial sort of stats oddity (e.g. "That was the first 'Circus Comes to Town' encore since 9/11/99"). There's the crowd that lives for the jam, those moments where Phish open themselves up to the improvisational gods and let them deliver the music to wherever it will go. There are even subsets within the jam seeking crowd. Some people seek out the dark sound effects laden performances, but there are also connoisseurs of the happy, energetic jams, the ones that frequently get called "Hose" [32] in setlists.

Look around the crowd during a deep jam and you'll see people in bliss and others sitting there bored. Some punch the sky during "Chalk Dust," others craft internal mocking dialogues about those who still love that song. It's not that one group is there for the music and the other is there for the drugs or some conflict between noobs or jaded vets. It's simply that Phish have a wide enough range of styles that parts of the show can be enjoyed by people with very different tastes. I'm sure there's even someone who laments that they no longer play jazz standards anymore.

All of that was a prelude to explain the following: I'm a huge Phish fan, one of the biggest out there. I've travelled around the country seeing them, sacrificing regular meals, warm beds and any sort of fiscal sanity and family harmony. I was at a concert that regularly gets described as one of Phish's best in their history, and I was bored. At one point I actually even thought about heading out early, but – of course – I never do that.

That was a lesson learned at my 4th Grateful Dead show. The Dead encored with the clichéd weekend call of "One More Saturday Night" and the more cynical fans headed out. All of those missed the "Ripple" second encore, the only time the Grateful Dead would play it after the acoustic 1981 "Oops" set[33] in Amsterdam. I had an amazing time while others sat out in the parking lot feeling smug about beating the rush. I got to learn that one the easy way. Never ever leave until the houselights come on.

---

[32] The term "Hose" comes from 1992 when Phish toured with Santana. He had an image that Phish was just a hose through which the music flowed, watering the audience, because we're – y'know – like flowers or something. Like or love the arboreal audience analogy, the idea of music flowing through the band, using them to manifest the notes instead of consciously creating it is a powerful image. I was in a weird band in college. I would tell stories over repetitive music. While we were called Plum(b) Awful for an all too apparent reason, even I had moments where I wouldn't know where the next sentence of the story was coming from, but it all worked in some bizarre way. The hose is a real thing.

[33] Called that because it was only played due to two other shows being canceled. It wasn't promoted and the band had to play with borrowed instruments as their real equipment was already being transported to their next scheduled concert as per the original plans.

I made my money on tour selling sodas in the lot, a job that requires being outside and ready for the post-show parched crowd. That didn't matter. I could venture towards the exit to get a quick start, but until the lights were on and the canned music was playing, I would stay inside. The important distinction is that I was vending to be able to see shows, not seeing shows in order to have a place to make a few dollars.

So while I didn't leave, I headed out towards the top of the Rocks. It's not exactly a hardship doing so. There's an incredible view of Denver to peruse and this wasn't some sort of 2004 style flub fest. Even if the concert isn't transcendental, there was far worse ways of spending a June evening than sitting in a beautiful theatre hearing Phish play a concert.

My reaction was not that unique. When I first heard the best show ever theory floated about this night, I went back to Google Groups' archive of rec.music.phish to see how people reacted in the moment. The answer is that they didn't. There was a lot of talk about some of the shows later in the month, but June 11 came and went to little response.

What caused the change is that this night was broadcast on KBOC. Since the broadcast wasn't on the night of the show, all of the Colorado tapers had time to get their gear set up and record it. There were years between this soundboard circulating and the Live Phish CD series. During that time, this night became the standard bearer for the era. There might not be much difference between 6/11/94 – a show that will always get mentions when the greatest show conversation is raised – and the completely forgotten 5/26/94, but this is less a vote for this night and more a statement of support for the era of playing. I might have moved on and been more curious about this new style that was emerging, but June 11 makes a perfectly good representative for early 1994 (and really a throwback towards 1993). It was a time of energy and precise playing. Even without the extended jams and pure improvisation, there were always incredible peaks. If you find yourself lacking recordings from this period, there are far worse places to start than the second night of the second year of Red Rocks.

13: JUNE 13, 1994 – MEMORIAL HALL
KANSAS CITY, KS

In which tour games are explained.

Going from Denver to eastern Kansas state line is pretty simple. You just would have to put your car into neutral and push. At least that was my joke leading up to that drive. You drop from 5280 feet to well under 1000 throughout the rolling hills of Kansas. What I was not prepared for was just how much rolling had to be done. The drive goes on for much longer than anyone should have to tolerate. It's 600 miles of pure tedium with few interesting towns or attractions to break it up.

I thought I had a rescue. I owned a copy of *Roadside America*, a book of oddball tourist attractions. Alas, even that failed me. The limitations of print meant that they didn't have space to include directions to these points of questionable interest. I was hoping to see the Atomic Cannon in Junction City, but there weren't exactly informational signs for that along the Interstate, at least not in 1994. When all else fails, there's always the rule of the power driver: Press on. Buy some gas, grab a snack, get back in the car. Miles to go before we jam.

The Kansas City that people think of when the Chiefs and Royals come to mind is actually in Missouri. You have to drive slightly west to get to the eponymous state. Memorial Hall was in a separate town just across the state line.

While this appears to not be so true now, at the time Kansas City, KS was a tad on the sketchy side. Missouri had a perfect strategy to keeping down their crime rate. Find a city on the other side of a state line with a similar enough name and hope it all goes there. Kansas City, KS, East St. Louis, IL, it was a perfect plan. The criminals would be too bewildered to rob them!

While I didn't actually experience any danger outside the venue, inside was starting to be another story. The opening combination of "Buried Alive > Poor Heart" gets dark. When people think about Phish and improvisation, the general focus is on what the fanbase calls Type 2 (or Type II) jams. The distinction between a Type 1 and Type 2 jam is in how closely they stick to the traditional structure of the song. "Chalk Dust Torture" has a mid song jam that (usually) is similar to other versions but with slight variations. The flip of that is "Tweezer" which could sound like anything ten minutes into the jam. The easiest way to describe the distinction between the two types is to have someone play you a mid-jam snippet that you've never heard before. If you can immediately identify the song, then it's Type 1.

At least for a subset of the Phish community, Type 2 jams get all of the attention. A show is good if and only if a large segment of the concert is spent outside of a structure of any song. The different categories are a useful distinction, especially for songs that very rarely have extended jams. If you refer to a show as having a "Type 2 Chalk Dust" or a "Type 2 AC/DC Bag," that's a quick way to express that the show could be a lot different than you'd expect just from perusing the setlist. The downside to this jargon is that language can structure our thoughts. When categories are created, we tend to think in terms of them. The Kansas City opening salvo reminds why it's wrong to interchange the ideas of Type 2 jamming and improvisation too carelessly.

"Buried Alive" isn't any longer than usual – the song clocks in at 2:38 and some of that track is cheering – and pretty much does what the song does, but there's one exception. Around the 1:30 mark of the song Trey starts messing with his guitar pedals and comes up with a unique effect, one that I don't think I've heard in any other show. It sounds like a bit like a UFO landing or a video game. It only gets engaged for twenty or thirty seconds, but it adds an additional touch of menace, perfect for an already stressful song. Much like "My Friend My Friend" has a rhythm perfect for stabbing someone and the jam section of "Maze" sounds like someone running through a labyrinth before they hit walls, "Buried Alive," would indeed make a perfect soundtrack for anyone unfortunate enough to find the earth rushing at them. A kindred effect is used during "My Sweet One" as Mike starts up his solo, giving a connection that songs of death and love so rarely have.

Death and love would be the themes of the night. A few songs later "Wolfman's Brother" would drop into a funk jam more akin to a 1997 version than what they performed in 1994. Channeling your future selves to that degree could cause a temporal paradox, so they quickly jumped into "Dinner and a Movie" rather than finishing the song. No more movie monsters, hurricanes, and ships running aground; now we're having date night. "Stash" – partially about a rogue policeman who doesn't just kill people, but gets annoyed when his victims have the nerve to treat their wound with good humor – gets played with heart stopping, terrifying abandon [34] but it's followed by "Ginseng Sullivan," a wistful ode to a man and his love of his "Muddy water Mississippi Delta home."

It continued in the second set. After a rather angry sounding "Mike's Song" with a brief return of the UFO effect – the jam was more like a "Split Open and Melt" or "Stash" than "Mike's." It no, are no, nice jam. – we had the classic "Mike's Groove" combination of "I Am Hydrogen" and "Weekapaug Groove."

"Weekapaug" is about "trying to make a woman that you move." That lyric might not make the most sense, but we're in the land of love, or at least the desire for it. That might be a stretch but the subsequent song was "Esther," a malicious ditty about an evil puppet that turns an entire town against a little girl. When its minions fail to off her, the felonious felt forces the issue and drowns her.

This accidental pairing was working so well that by the middle of the second set, they were getting both themes into a single song. "Reba" is a song about creating meat – death – but artificial meat, one that reduces killing – animal love! – but the ingredients require parts of a horse and worms – death!. This was followed by the ultimate mixing that is "Jesus Just Left Chicago." More than anyone Jesus's life was defined by those two. There used to be a trend at football games for people to sit behind the end zone and hold up a sign during extra point and field goal attempts. Their goal was to spread

---

[34] If there's no other lesson I hope you get from this book, I hope you download and listen to every single "Stash" and "Split Open and Melt" from Summer 94. The space they all go to is similar but they're all amazing and just different enough to make them all worthwhile.

the gospel of Christianity. With only one a tiny piece of poster board to sum up a great world religion, they settled on writing "John 3:16." For God so loved the world that he gave his one and only Son, so that whoever believes in him shall not perish and have eternal life. Love, death, death, love, and driving through Mississippi. Love and death, love and death, what else is there to sing about?

There used to be a vendor who would drive up to Bard from New York City and set up cassette holders filled with concert bootlegs. We could all get Grateful Dead recordings on our own, but there was no other way to hear different artists, so a lot of us scrounged up the $8. One of my purchases was a Suzanne Vega bootleg from her club days. She used to love telling stories before each song. One my favorites introduced a song that never did stick around. A friend of hers informed her that all of her songs were either about love or mental health. She was flummoxed to find a different topic until inspiration finally struck. If her old standbys were to be denied, she'd write a little ditty called "The Rent Song." Alas, while the intent was there, it turned out to be another mental health.

Phish might have had a few outs along those lines but they chose a different approach for their encore. They brought the whole idea down to its core component. What are love and death if not the building blocks of biology? The perfect encore for the night would be "Golgi Apparatus."

According to the credits on my original cassette of *Junta*, "Golgi Apparatus" was "written in 8th grade by the immortal songwriting team of Szuter, Woolfe [sic], Marshal [sic], and Anastasio."[35] You could probably figure that, because it sounds like the sort of song some intelligent – but bored – kids would come up with when hearing words like "golgi apparatus" and "lysosome." Like many songs created in a middle school environment, they sound cool but make little sense. In fact, the lyrics are so nonsensical that they managed to go through the other side and become deep again. It's

---

[35] Yes, the liner notes misspelled the names of two of the writers, giving Aaron "Not Errand" Woolf an extra e at the expense of taking an l away from Tom Marshall. It would be nice to blame a record studio here, but these tapes were self produced. Of course, seeing how this book is self-published, I had best be careful about my mockery.

difficult to request my bank balance without thinking that I'm looking into my finance box just to check my status. Thank you Bored Boys of Biology for infecting me with that for life.

What makes this song is the hook. Twice – one of which is even more effective as it comes out of an stunning instrumental section that builds to a great peak before dropping into it: tension and release at its finest. – there's an anthemic singing of, "I saw you with a ticket stub in your hand." That might not be breathless poetry, but it's surprisingly liberating to reach into your pocket and pull out a stub and wave it around.

On this tour, I was wearing an old Guatemalan vest as part of my outfit. The idea of having a standard outfit was something I picked up from watching Doctor Who; I started it in college and continued during the college-esque environment that is being on the road. I kept all of my old stubs in my vest pocket. When they got to that line, it wasn't enough to pull out a ticket and hold it up; I had to go through the stack and find one from a venue at least two time zones away. It's not as though anyone else would notice me doing this. It was solely a game I was playing to amuse myself.

Zzyzx Tour Lesson Number Seven: *When you see multiple shows on a tour, there will always be a song or two that just isn't doing it for you. One trick to make it through that and enjoy it anyway is to figure out some sort of game or joke or dance that you can do. If you focus your energy on that instead of "Character Zero?' Again? Really?" you can find that you're more ready to enjoy the songs that you actually like.*

That was something I did a lot in early shows. I came up with these games and tricks and jokes, thinking that they were just a way for me to have in jokes for one and no one else would notice. Was I usually up against the rail when I was doing these? Well yeah. Right between Mike and Trey was a great spot to stand. It was amazing to watch Trey's fingers move with precision faster than I could move mine randomly. Sure I was so close to the stage in those pre-barrier days that I regularly used the edge as a resting spot for my clipboard, but it's not like this would be an issue, right? Right?

14: JUNE 14, 1994 – CIVIC CENTER DES MOINES, IA

Years of band interaction come to a somewhat inevitable end.

One of the bonuses of seeing Phish before they became the international superstars that they are today was that the four of them would just hang out before and after shows. Go to enough shows, and you were bound to meet up with them. Fortunately, they all happen to be nice and interesting people. Had they no musical talent at all, they'd still be people you'd look for at shows to get their reactions to the music and the crowd.

I have to confess that I'm really reluctant to put these stories into print. I never have posted any of these to online forums or emails or anything. These events all happened in passing here and there throughout the years, and none of them were in the context of me writing a book. I didn't want to be the guy who used them to move more ink.

Why am I writing them? Well it helps that the only person who comes across as being annoying and stupid in these stories is me. I don't have tales of debauchery or the like, just soon to be rock stars having to deal with an obsessed fan. Also the band itself has told the central story in past interviews; that seems to make it fair game. Most importantly though, there is no way to write a book about summer 1994 and my adventures across the country without going into details about the night of June 14 and what happened in a Des Moines parking lot.[36]

---

[36] I needed to check the details of the spelling of Aaron Woolf's name for the previous chapter, so I contacted Phish's lyricist Tom Marshall. He confirmed that there was no "e" in the end of it. I explained to him why I needed to know this and told him my dilemma about publishing off the record stories. He encouraged – nay, demanded!- that these be told, "You have to TELL THE STORIES!"

My first shows didn't happen in the Midwest of course. They were all centered around upstate New York. I would go down to The Chance in Poughkeepsie and the Capitol Theatre in Port Chester, north to Aiko's in Saratoga, or east to many venues around Northampton, MA. It was easy to see the band a couple dozen times between 1989 and 1991 if you had the energy of youth and were situated in the Hudson Valley.

The scene was small enough then that band members would start to notice you if you kept returning. It started out slowly. I was introduced to Fishman. I had some conversations with then head of merchandise Bob "Claw Me Down" Smith. He remembered me and put me in charge of the merchandise at the Aiko's show when a fuse blew during "The Ballad of Curtis Loew." Jon walked by me in The Chance parking lot when I was listening to a tape of "The Mango Song" and remarked, "Hey, I know that song!"

I continued to go to shows and our conversations got more elaborate. The turning point was when I drove 140 miles in February of 1990 to buy an album. Their concert a few shows prior was billed as a release party for *Lawn Boy*. I loved *Junta* enough that I couldn't wait. I went up the Taconic State Parkway and over the Mass Pike to get to U Mass Amherst. As soon as I arrived, I found Claw Me Down and asked for a copy. He told me that he only had one left, but he'd sell it to me because I drove so far. I was excited to get it a few days early, but it turned out more than that. This wasn't just the last copy that they had that day. It was the final remaining self-produced tape that they ever sold. They had signed with Absolute A Go Go. The album was finally officially released in September but for months I was the only Bard student to have a copy. Since no one else could get it, I figured it was ok for me to make copies for people.

There was only one problem. The album is 47 minutes long. Most people

---

He also demanded that he get a paragraph. Unfortunately, I didn't really start interacting with Tom until around 2000 and this is a book about 1994. If I can't tell Tom Marshall stories, I can do the next best thing. I'm making him my scapegoat. Jon, Trey, Mike, Page: if you don't like this chapter, blame Tom. I wouldn't have written it without his encouragement.

Disclaimer: while I'm using quotes here, it's been over 20 years for these stories. I'm probably getting the exact words wrong. Artistic license.

used 90-minute tapes to trade. A XL-90 really had about 45:30 – 46:30 worth of recording time on a side, but it never was quite enough to fit the entire album. I couldn't just duplicate the sides of the album, because the 20 minutes of blank space on each time would annoy the listener; yet another failing of cassettes as a medium is that they made it difficult to skip to the next song or the next side. Blank space had to be fast forwarded through, which could take some time. I would either had to come up with filler, waste a lot of tape, or find another solution.

During the period between self-release and A Go Go, I talked to Page before a show. It amused me to complain about the difficulty about stealing their music so I explained my dilemma about the 47-minute album and the 45-minute sides of tape. "So what did you do?" he asked. Well I cut "Lawn Boy" off of tapes.

"Wait a minute. *I* sing that!" I tried to explain that it wasn't personal and thought I was making progress until he pointed out the alternative solution, "'Oh Kee Pah!' You could cut 'Oh Kee Pah!' out and it would fit." The answer of, "Well I like 'The Oh Kee Pah Ceremony,'" failed to soothe the issue somehow. He walked away.

Later I ran into him again and jokingly asked him to buy me a shirt. He didn't have any cash and besides, "I don't buy shirts for people who cut 'Lawn Boy' off of tapes."

Not everything was so dramatic of course. Trey and Mike would answer questions. Page gave me shit; a full year later, I suggested a song option for the evening. "I don't make the setlists," he replied, "and besides I don't take requests from people who cut 'Lawn Boy' off of tapes." For the most part, I felt pretty happy with my relationship with the band. So I did what obsessives do. I sat down and wrote a letter.

I wrote a long letter. I wrote a long letter asking many nitpicky questions. I wrote a long letter asking many nitpicky questions that I carefully numbered. I wrote a long letter asking many nitpicky questions that I carefully numbered, using internal dialogue for parts of songs that only I would understand (e.g. referring to "The second part of 'Divided Sky'" (the part that now has a long pause), or wondering why they no longer played the ending to "Wilson." The last one is especially bad as there was no different arrangement that had been dropped. Rather it was a cover of the Frank Zappa instrumental "Peaches en Regalia" that no one bothered to label on my tape.)

A few months later, I received a reply. The response was amazing. Trey mailed back my paper with notes below my questions like, "I have no idea what you're talking about." I'm pretty sure at least a dozen of the points were answered in that way. I would love to quote from it to demonstrate just how annoying a young male with a new musical obsession can be to artists, but – alas – I lost this letter decades ago in one of my many moves.

Not all of my band interactions had the dynamic of my incredibly cringe worthy behavior being handled surprisingly well. There was a period there where Trey knew I wanted to hear "Punch You in the Eye" so he wouldn't play it at any show I attended. Mike once gave an incredible response to being asked how he dealt with songs that he was temporarily sick of: "Part of my job is to act excited, even if I'm not." That's a lesson that I've taken throughout my working life. "Sure, that task you just gave me sounds fascinating!" I asked if various songs would be brought back, was invariably told that they were dead, only to have them return a few years later. The only time that the response was, "Yeah, I've been thinking about playing that one again," was for "No Dogs Allowed." That was 1992 and it still hasn't happened.

Still though, the fact is that young males – and especially young males who are busy studying graduate level mathematics – are not always known for their social skills. I was always at least self-aware enough to know that I'm not always self-aware so one important rule was created.

Zzyzx Tour Lesson Number Eight: *Always give the band members a way out when you're talking with them. They will always be far more fascinating to you than you will be to them. Remember that and try to make sure that they can always escape if you're annoying them. I was always careful to try to not overstay my welcome but see above re young math geeks and their ability to interact successfully with others. I didn't know it, but*

I was heading for a conflict.

Every city needs something to distinguish itself. Sure it's the capitol of Iowa and has a very active river pouring through its heart, but Des Moines tends to be forgotten. Most cities have some cool nickname to call it by. What does Des Moines get? Apparently the city mainly goes by "DSM." When you're forced to use your airport code, it doesn't make people rush to buy plane tickets. They do have a secondary nickname based on their insurance industry roots: Hartford of the West. I can see the ad campaign now. "Come to Des Moines! It's just like Hartford, only in the Central Time Zone!" Des Moines needed a way to create an identity and in the mid 90s they thought they had found it.

They would build skybridges. Lots and lots of skybridges! You can walk for four miles around Des Moines without ever having to cross a street or go outside. They even tried to get the nickname "City of Skywalks." Maybe it's time for the *Roadside America* authors to stage an intervention and get them to build the world's largest Ear of Corn, lest people ask themselves, "Is this tedium? No, this is Iowa." Right now the largest ear is in Oliva, Minnesota. Where's your Iowan pride?

However, Des Moines had not yet gotten out their maize. I tried to spend the hours before the show wandering the skywalks but that was just about as exciting as you think it would be. Besides, it was way too nice of a day to spend in sealed passages. Hanging out by the venue was a better idea for one reason: the tribes were starting to gather.

After traveling solo for weeks, it was a great change of pace to have others along for company. Shorter drives lowered the barrier to stay on tour, leading to more people hitting the road. The lot now featured Amy "Wheelitzo" Caygill. She had a letter published in the brand new Schvice asking for a nickname to replace her "lame excuse of a name." Wheelitzo was Mike's helpful suggestion. When that happens you just have to run with it. There also was the woman who had the big crush on Mike who spent her afternoons bantering with the one who preferred Page over which one was more important to the music on a given night. There were a few tapers and vendors and the Greenpeace crew. It might have not been the Grateful Dead lot, but it was large enough to be interesting without attracting the problems that lurked with the bigger group.

While I largely fell out of touch with this group – if there's one task the Internet has perfected, it's letting nomadic people who had an amazing few weeks together turn a fun memory into a lifelong connection, but social media wasn't even a concept yet – it made a huge difference having kindred spirits along for the journey. It's hard enough to explain being part of a subculture. When you're the only one around driving long distances to see a band over and over again, it's easy to start questioning yourself. Being part of a group of people also doing this feels much saner.

With validation comes conversation. On a tour as great as this one was, there was plenty for us to discuss, compare, and contrast. When that got old, there were some interesting fountains across the street from the venue. Did we avail ourselves of the chance to wash off the dust from the road? Of course not! That would be wrong.

It wasn't all skybridges and fountains. There was a show to be played! After an energetic "Llama" opener we had a weird moment, one involving the song "Guelah Papyrus." "Guelah" is a throwback to the song writing patterns of Phish's early days in that the middle section of the song originally appeared as a standalone instrumental titled "The Asse Festival." After it joined forces with a set of lyrics, the structure was set. The first two verses would be sung followed by "The Asse Festival." Then there would be a long pause. A pause – much like this one – designed to heighten your anticipation, to make you long for the rest of the song to finish, to – if it really went on and on and on – make you want to do anything to make it stop and the rest of the song continue. Once again: tension and release, the hallmark of Phish. Finally they'd sing, "So maybe I could be a fly," and the song would continue.

This version started out normally enough but then diverged. The pause led to a non-amplified version of "Sweet Adeline." Yes, that "Sweet Adeline." The barbershop quartet classic was a standard in the early 90s. It was sung over 125 times between 1991 and 1994, but only once did it appear in the middle of "Guelah Papyrus." The unusual pause created a brief moment of confusion as to where to go from there. A brief digital delay loop jam ensued before they finally concluded the song.

That's how this show went. There are some nights that have endless, elaborate improvisations that standout but others are subtler. There's a brief jam out of the "Fee" before it resolves into "My Friend My Friend." The usual vacuum or trombone solo in the middle of "I Didn't Know" was replaced with another unamplified song; it was "My Sweet One" this time. Song sandwiches are not very common in general. Getting two in one set, both in songs not known for setlist oddities, was at least interesting.

If the theme of the show is good improvisation can come in small timing packages, the best example might be the "Split Open and Melt." Clocking in at 9:38, it was short for a 1994 version – of the 10 versions I saw this summer, only 6/11 was shorter and many were over 14 minutes – but what it did was concentrate its intensity. I've been known to argue that this was the best "Melt" of the summer; in fact I would mention that in my defense a couple days later… but that gets ahead of the story.

Where does this story start? It's not in the second set opening "Frankenstein," or the very sweet "If I Could" or even in the "You Enjoy Myself" with its cool jam on "On Broadway" – Trey first hit a riff similar to the theme between verses, then he played the vocal melody to the song. The band then picked up on it and kept it going for a second go round. At that point the crowd started singing along to Trey's playing and clapping to Fishman's beat. Sometimes teases are a brief riff, but others are a two minute fun jam – which was later continued in Mike's solo and then the vocal jam. Let's jump to right after the "YEM."

As usually happens before a Fishman section, Argent's "Hold Your Head Up" was played. In case people didn't know why they use that song, Jon made it clear in the introduction as he sang, "I hate this song/I hate this song/You know I hate this song," over the riff. Sure, some bands operate out of mutual respect of the likes of each other, but how many of them stick around for three decades?

Jon sung Syd Barrett's "Bike," giving its important lyrics the serious devotion that they deserve, delivered his vacuum solo, and took a few laps as the "Hold Your Head Up" outro played. He then ran up to the front of the stage to high five people in the front row. As always, I was situated between Mike and Trey up against the stage; the security barrier with the rail wouldn't come along until after the theatre stage. As Fishman came up to our section, a man in the second row checked me into the stage as he reached forward to try to touch the drummer's hand.

It was actually a scary moment how violent (albeit accidentally) that motion was. It took me a few seconds to regain my breath after that. As "Possum" started, one that would continue the "On Broadway" theme, I rolled my eyes at the fan behind me and thought, "Oh my God! You got to touch Jon Fishman's hand for a tenth of a second! That's totally worth squashing people!" This gesture, one that I thought was only for me, would have consequences.

Zzyzx Tour Lesson Number Nine: *This is an important corollary to Tour Lesson Number Seven! Shows give the impression of anonymity but it's just an illusion. If you're up front, the band has no choice but to look at you. An in-joke for yourself can actually be seen by them and they can interpret it quite differently than you intended.*

After the Sample encore, I walked back into the night and spent a little time outside the venue. The further east the tour went, the more people hopped on board. There was a day off after Des Moines, so no one was really in a hurry to make the short drive to Minneapolis. That's why there was a crowd milling about when I was approached by Brad Sands.

Brad Sands was Phish's road manager for years. He's probably best known in the Phish community for a clip in the Phish documentary *Bittersweet Motel* where Trey throws an empty beer can at him and calls him a fucking tool, but he served a useful role in the organization. Among other jobs, he was the professional bad cop. It was his job to turn down requests and otherwise handle the less pleasurable aspects of being public personas.

Sometimes a barrier between the band and the fans is a good thing. If Trey shoots you down, you can have some resentment. If it's Brad, the two of you can bond over how he's a jerk and it sucks that he's making these rules, but what can you do, you know? So that's why it was Brad who got the duty of approaching me and saying – rather bluntly – that the band hates it when I stand in the front row timing songs. It's not just that it annoyed them. I was actually ruining shows by doing so.

That – more than anything – is what I remember from this night. Phish was my escape at this time. I spent my free time driving around the country, because their music let me forget about grad school and how broke I was and how ill suited for a liberal vegetarian southern New Mexico was in the early 1990s. Shows had those moments where the only thing that existed in the world was the music. It's the closest thing to a religious experience I have had. And I was performing the same role that always happens. I was taking the ineffable and trying to bring it back to the world, to document the experience as best I could. Reason always seems to lead to the destruction of the mystical.

It's a rough moment to be told that you were destroying the very thing that you love the most. Right after Brad left, someone asked me how I felt about him bitching me out. I couldn't even answer the question. Here I was, sleeping in my car, eating cold ravioli – and having days where I couldn't even afford that; the road can get rough sometimes – doing whatever I could to see this band because their music brought me that much joy. To be informed that I was wrecking it, that the very essence of who I am was making it that much harder for the music to exist... well how do you think it would make me feel? I stood around in a daze for a while. Then Brad came back. "Trey wants to talk to you," he said and walked me onto the tour bus.

Phish having a tour bus was a relatively new thing in their world. Transportation was a bit more haphazard in the early 90s. I once saw Page drive up to the Capitol Theatre in a rather unreliable looking 1970s boat of car. On 2/10/90 Phish was reduced to begging for a ride back home to Burlington from the Philadelphia area; the pre-"Carolina" request is especially amusing, "Fish's proverbial engine has died!" Having long road trips can be a bonding experience, or at least give you funny material to base the Watkins

Glens' "Colonel Forbin's Ascent" story around, but as the venue size grew, the importance of being refreshed (and making sure that they and their equipment made it to the show for that matter) increased. It was on the 1992 I-64 mini summer tour of Norfolk, Charlottesville, and Richmond – the brief interlude between the H.O.R.D.E. tour and the long series of shows opening for Carlos Santana – that they first rode up like an actual touring project. Trey was apologetic about the bus, telling those in the lot that he knew it might make it harder for us to be able to keep up with the tour as they could now cover greater distances, but I think everyone understood it was for the good. June 14 was the only time I was actually on the bus. I would describe it in great detail, explain where the chess games happened and where Page played Tetris, but I never actually made it past the drivers' area. The rest was behind another door. Like everything in the rock world, there is always an additional level that you can be excluded from seeing.

The advantage of having Brad as the enforcer is that it freed up Trey to be the nice guy. What did he have to say to me? It wasn't that big of a deal. When Trey is on stage, he doesn't want to think about anything, and I was making him think about the time of songs. It was all completely understandable and I stayed away from the front row for years; the next time I ventured there was summer 2000 where I had a photo pass for Jambands.com at Deer Creek, which I got in part to play a joke on the band. See? I'm in front of the first row now!

There are only two things that I really remember from the conversation. The first is that halfway through, someone came onboard and announced that the Rangers had won the Stanley Cup. I'm probably the only non-fan to know exactly where he was when the Rangers broke their 54-year curse. The second was that Trey wanted to talk a lot about how they chose what song to play, about how rarities are fun, but they could be inspired to play a song like "Sample" for the encore.

I didn't know why he thought that was an important point to raise until the next show. It turns out what angered the band and brought everything to a head wasn't the timing. Remember when I rolled my eyes at the guy who just *had* to touch Jon's hand? That was interpreted as a complaint about the "Possum" song selection. It was much easier to abandon my post up front once that sunk in. I root for songs and for directions of jams and come up with ways to keep myself entertained when there's a song that currently isn't my favorite, and that's all well and good, but the front row is best populated by those who are so excited to be there that it inspires the band to play harder. Going up front every night makes it just another place to be. Now that I venture to the rail once a year or so, the excitement of being there overwhelms my internal monologue. Then again, finding ways to still have the fresh ears for the music when it's your 10th show of the tour or the 100th of your life is the struggle of tour.

Sometimes that challenge is met not by the music as much as the incidents that occurred. 6/14/94 might not be the best night of music of the tour, but it was one of the least forgettable one, for me personally and for the stories that get told years later. In honor of that, here's a present to you Des Moines. A major event in a very small community happened here. Embrace it. Build a giant functional stopwatch. Put up signs saying, "Welcome to Des Moines where The Timer was banned from the front row!" Have residents say, "I'm from Des Moines, you can't time me!" Sure, only a few dozen people would get it, but it's still better than City of Skywalks.

15: JUNE 16, 1994 – STATE THEATRE MINNEAPOLIS, MN

Aftermath

A day off. A day off with less than 250 miles to drive. We weren't out west anymore. Time had to be killed. In my case, I went to Clear Lake, IA to try to find the venue where Buddy Holly performed his last concert before the day the music died. I was a huge fan of Bradley Denton's bizarre novel about the power of Rock and Roll *Buddy Holly Is Alive and Well on Ganymede,* so I thought that might make a good pilgrimage. Alas, once again I could not find my destination so I searched out a different god. I headed north on I-35W[37] and went to the Mall of America in Bloomington, MN. It had just opened a few years prior and was still used as a metaphor for what was wrong with consumerism. I wanted to see the place that could turn Adam Smith into a Marxist, but I wasn't so much repelled as bored.

How do you fill a giant four-story mall? They had multiple outlets for the same vendor. We didn't know it at the time, but the Mall of America didn't point out the failings of 20th century capitalism as much as it pointed to the woes of the early 21st. The enemy is no longer consumption as much as it is homogenization. No matter where you go, you always have the same stores, the same restaurants, and the same culture. Who knew that a shrine to consumerism created after the greed of the 80s would actually be ahead of its

---

[37] The "W" in that route number stands for west. The highway system used to have many split Interstates; for example I-84 from Utah to Portland used to be known as I-80N and the road to San Francisco was I-80S. The Interstate System eliminated all of these to prevent motorist confusion. The two remaining ones are both on I-35; it splits between Dallas and Ft. Worth and Minneapolis and St. Paul. One reason the numbering was allowed to remain was so neither of these city pairs would be considered the lesser of the two by getting a spur route instead of the main one. You got your politics in my naming convention!

time?

This show was a bizarre experience for me. Des Moines had ended oddly but I had a day to think about things and accept that it was just OK to stand further back in the crowd and enjoy from a different vantage point. However, as I was looking for a spot to stand pre-show, another fan approached me and said that Trey absolutely hated me being at shows and I should just drop off tour. While it turned out that it was just a garbled version of the message that Brad eventually successfully delivered, I spent the night pondering my future with this band and if I should continue seeing them. Had I known the venue size increase that was about to come, I wouldn't have had to worry in the slightest – you can't annoy the band from the 200 level of Madison Square Garden - but I can't say that this is a show that I enjoyed much.

That's too bad as it has a lot going for it. The first set has an intense "Maze," a bizarre combination of "The Curtain" and "Dog Faced Boy," the latter played completely straight for a change. Most of the other versions from the summer had Fishman stand on the front of the stage and make funny faces as an "emotion solo." There also was yet another ridiculously amazing "Stash." This one doesn't slow down for one second during the jam. The energy is focused like how a fire hose can turn a spray of water into a powerful weapon. Please only use the 6/16/94 "Stash" for peaceful purposes.

The second set – while a bit disjointed – would have two moments of lasting importance. One of them was a theme for the rest of the summer. Phish have a non-song named "Kung." It's a chant with immortal lines such as, "Kang well in martin land/Fervent fourth/ Mere Fervent fifth." It was recited twice in 1989 – in consecutive shows no less - and then was abandoned seemingly forever before its return in 12/31/92. It made a few appearances in 1993, but they weren't quite sure what to do with it. However, on this night in Minneapolis a new potential purpose was found for the song. "Kung" wasn't a bizarre poem Fishman wrote. Instead it was magical words from the *The Helping Friendly Book* that – when recited – would transport you into Gamehendge. "Kung" continued to be used as part of story songs throughout the summer. That was just a phase for it though. It would eventually return to being a random connector, useful for either launching a jam into weirdness or to try to return from a jamming abyss.

The second change was more lasting. After a rather interesting "Big Ball Jam," one that was closer to the dark intensity of a "Stash" jam than the usual random plinks on strings, "Down With Disease" started. This version would point to the future. The twenty-nine previous versions of the song followed a predictable albeit enjoyable pattern in their jam sections. Trey would play the most infectious riff ever, there would be a high-energy jam for two or three minutes, and then they'd return to the theme. Minneapolis received a different approach.

As soon as the main riff was finished, there was an immediate departure from the norm. Trey played a theme reminiscent of the Steve Miller Band's "Swingtown." After fooling around with that for a few minutes, Page led the jam into a quieter space, an area very infrequently explored by the previous "Down With Diseases." There was a brief stab at returning to the "Cannonball" theme that worked so well in Dallas a month prior, and then Trey played the introduction to "Contact" over the jam. The segue happened and for the first time ever "Down With Disease" was marked "unfinished" in the setlist. Over the years, this song would evolve into a major force for improvisation. Jams would spiral out of the tune, never to return. The next time you listen to an extended "Down With Disease" jam, remember that it all came out of a slightly elongated version from Minneapolis.

While I didn't know the historic moment I had just witnessed, it was interesting enough to pull me out of my funk. As much as I like the individual members of the band, as much fun as the travel is, as many friends as I've met over the years, it's those brief minutes where the music is so powerful that the rest of the world disappears that keep me returning. For those who have never experienced that power, it's hard to describe, but it's euphoric, spiritual, and as addictive as any drug.

My life would be so much easier in some ways – most notably financially – if I didn't feel the pull of music so strongly, but music was (and still is) my lifeline. As a mathematician and a programmer, I spend most of my days enslaved to logic and reason. It's crucial to be able to leave that state, even if it's just for a few minutes during a brief jam. If nothing else, escaping my normal thought patterns makes them so much clearer and stronger when I return to them. Many of my best ideas have happened after the conclusion of a great jam when everything is sharper. If there was ever a night I needed this reminder, it was this one. No, I wasn't happy that I was annoying people I liked, people who made the very experience I needed possible, but there was indeed a reason why I continued to attend.

The band came out for the encore and played "Ginseng Sullivan" with no amplification. Trey then promised (or threatened, depending on your tastes) to play one naked. There then was this banter.

Trey: This next song is very long, very long

Jon: Days

Trey: Dave, this one's for you, it's a long song.

Audience tapes of the unamplified material can be a frustrating listen. The levels had to be turned up as high as they could go. This means that any crowd noise becomes incredibly loud. In this case though, I'm always brought back to the moment. My laugh is clearly audible on the recording as all of the tension of the past 48 hours was released.

The days long song turned out to be "Amazing Grace." That somehow seemed appropriate. Sure, a "no hard feelings" moment isn't exactly the same as having a messiah appear to forgive all of our transgressions and prevent us from experiencing eternal torment, but at least I no longer felt quite so Satanic.

I hung out afterward to talk to band. I apologized for being such an anal-retentive math geek. They reassured me that the likelihood of actually filing that restraining order was relatively low. Still though, reflecting on this night makes me ask the question of if I would trade. If I could go through it all again, would I do so as someone better adjusted, one who saw the shows, clapped his hands – perhaps channeling an inner British cricket fan and screaming, "Well played, boys!" after a particularly good jam – and went home? The answer is a resounding no.

Yes, this low was bad, but the highs were equally intense. A dedication from the stage, having a song partially written about me for the 9/22/99 soundcheck,[38] having my mathematical expertise tapped to create an album cover for the Trey solo project *18 Steps*[39], none of these happen without the more frustrating moments. Sometimes you have to play to your strengths, even if they're being a weird math geek.

---

[38] This was their second – and to date final – show in Las Cruces. I hadn't been back there since I moved to Seattle in 1995. Their tour manager Richard Glasgow (aka "Dicky Scotland") also was an alumnus of New Mexico State. They wrote a little song about him, in which it also was mentioned that the song just wouldn't be through unless they mentioned that The Timer was an Aggie too. It's a pretty funny song all around with the great couplet, "We love to see him/We love per diem."

[39] *18 Steps* was a companion item for the album *Bar 17*. Since they both involved numbers, Trey was curious to see if I could come up with a way of connecting the two. I cracked open my old math textbooks and came up with a convoluted way to get from 17 to 18 using 18 steps. An explanation of the math is available at http://www.jambands.com/columns/david-steinberg-some-are-mathematicians/2006/09/17/everyone-must-add-and-subtract-those-18-steps

16: JUNE 17, 1994 – EAGLES BALLROOM MILWAUKEE, WI

A field day for the heat.

If you go to a weather web site and look up the records for Milwaukee, you'll see that the record high for June 17 was 94 degrees set in 1994. While 94 doesn't sound that appallingly hot, throw in some humidity and it gets worse. Still though, at most you should have a day that's a tad on the frustrating side. Unfortunately this show was at the Eagles Ballroom, and that venue was completely unsuited for the task at hand.

The venue space was on the second story of a brick building with inadequate air conditioning. The only windows that could be opened were very small and at the top of the high ceiling so no air flow could possibly happen. How awful were the conditions? I spent the entire first set walking to and from the bathroom. I'd go to the sink, fill my hat with cold water, put in on my head, and go back out. That would cool me off for a minute or two but then I'd have to repeat it. It's pretty amazing that the band didn't collapse from the lights on stage. Yes they had a few fans aimed at them, but that wasn't likely to dispel enough of the oppressiveness.

The gold standard for heat and humidity for most Phish fans is Camp Oswego in summer 1999. That was ridiculously hot; my days were spent wandering out of my friends' shade structure only far enough to get to the frozen lemonade stand nearby. Even still, most of the shows were conducted after the sun went down and it was reasonably sane in the field. Milwaukee was less bad during the day, but the way the building absorbed all of the heat made this a worse experience. This first set is one of the few that are definitely more enjoyable to listen to on tape than it was to experience live.

This also might be true of the second set, but that's for a different reason.

It would be quite different today. During the setbreak, we'd all be playing with our phones and Facebook and Twitter would be ablaze about this insane car chase between O.J. Simpson and the police[40]. Never mind the Internet, in 1994 we couldn't even receive a phone call. When Phish came back on stage, none of us knew why the words "White Bronco" were suddenly relevant. In fact what with being on the road mostly listening to tapes with an occasional break to scan for local radio stations while finding a new one, for the longest time, I thought it was O.J. who was murdered. All we knew is that Phish was on stage, "Also Sprach Zarathustra" was the opener, it had finally cooled down a little inside the venue[41] , and Phish was screaming, "Run O.J. Run!" for some reason.

If that happens in one song, it could be random Phish wackiness, but it continued. "Poor Heart" also had Jon exhorting Simpson to make haste. "Mike's Song" went into a "Mission Impossible" jam with Fishman saying lines like, "Will he make it?" and "O.J. is heading for the airport. His only chance, his only chance is to run through the airport." The only people in the crowd who got the joke were the band members, but incomprehensibility can be its own reward.

This isn't to say that everything was lost on us in attendance. "Mike's" quickly resolved into the second ever "Simple." Those of us who were at The Warfield (or who had heard the tapes) were delighted. This version is perhaps the least anarchistic of the summer proto-"Simples" but it had its own spin on the tune. First there was the inevitable O.J. verse:

---

[40] For younger readers who only know O.J. Simpson through vague memories of this event, before this happened, Simpson was a famous football player who was in ads and even some movies. Imagine if Peyton Manning were suddenly accused of killing his ex-wife and led cops on a nationally televised, low-speed car chase around L.A., and you'd have the beginnings of understanding what this was like for those of us then. You'd also have to factor in that O.J. is an African American and Los Angeles still had a lot of distrust of the colorblindness of their police force due to still recent filming ad airing of footage of them beating an unarmed African American named Rodney King. There's reasons why this fascinated people, well at least those of us who weren't sitting at set break in an overheated ballroom.

[41] According to reviews on Phish.net, it was apparently still insanely warm near the stage. Those poor souls who didn't have the foresight to get banned from the front row in Des Moines found themselves at risk of collapsing from heat exhaustion.

"We've got O.J. (O.J.!)

'Cause we've got a band

And we've got O.J. in the band (O.J.! Run O.J.!)

What is a band without O.J. (O.J., O.J.!)?

O.J. is grand!"

The full verse was enough to end that joke (other than one exceedingly quick reference later), but it started up a new one. During "I Am Hydrogen," Phish played and sang "Simple" very slowly. It was one part "Hydrogen," one part "Simple," one part foreshadowing the Columbus show to come five days later. In addition to the pace, "I Am Simply Hydrogen" is worth listening to for some really low singing. It almost sounds as though a Tibetan monk is on stage.

So the set had some random screaming about O.J., it had two versions of the song that would become "Simple," this clearly was going to be a silly banter kind of show. In that case, what song works better than the holy grail of silliness: "Harpua?"

This "Harpua" didn't exist in a vacuum. Two references to other Phish events were made. First, as was done in Minneapolis, "Kung" was again chanted to bring us into Gamehendge. Other than its first two appearances, this is the only time that "Kung" was performed in consecutive concerts. Secondly Trey addressed the issue of the temperature as he said the following.

"Gamehendge is always covered with sort of a foggy haze, everywhere you look is a foggy haze. And it seems, the weather there is so cool and breezy and beautiful all the time that sometimes your mind plays tricks on you and you might actually start thinking that you're hot and sweaty but really in reality you're cool and warm and beautiful. It's just an illusion. And as soon as your mind, as soon as your mind overcomes that problem you suddenly realize that you're not hot and sweaty at all. You're actually out on a breezy wonderful day and the breeze is blowing over you. Ah, can you feel it?"

The mind over matter trick was only so successful, but it was probably worth a try.

The story didn't end there though. We learned that the reason that the evil old man hated the residents of the town was that they all liked to sing "Simple," (which was then called "The We've Got it Simple Song") and that Trey couldn't come up with a realistic town name for Jimmy and Poster Nutbag to live in on the fly. We discovered that Jimmy was a fan of Jimi... Hendrix that is, as Phish played a few seconds of "Voodoo Chile (Slight Return)" over the story.

Despite the new notes, this really is a classic version of "Harpua." There was a long buildup to the reveal of Poster Nutbag's name. The story was just about the fight. Versions after this became more about the random song played in the middle - the brief teases slowly evolved to become full covers of whatever song Jimmy was listening to - or some random story that would eventually have a quick mention of Jimmy and a cat shoehorned in at the end. My first show doesn't circulate but this is about as close to that moment that exists.

If you're curious about it, do not walk to the Internet to download it. Run, reader, run![42]

---

[42] Speaking of this "Harpua" and tapes, a great story circulates about this show. I didn't witness this in person, so I'm leaving it as a footnote. While Phish allows taping in a section behind the soundboard, some people swear that being in front of the soundboard – what are known as FOB recording, short for "Front of Board" – produces better recordings. Apparently, someone was running a FOB rig at this show but they weren't being as stealthy as they thought they were. Brad saw them and waited and waited and waited. The axe fell as "Harpua" started. Nothing crueler than tapus interruptus.

17: JUNE 18, 1994 – UIC PAVILION CHICAGO, IL

Capitalism meets mysticism and become friends for life.

There reaches a point in any tour where resources get stretched. That's part of the adventure of living on the road, but it's rarely fun when its happening. No looking into finance boxes was going to change my status. It didn't help that the tour was bringing us to expensive cities, ones that didn't like the idea of road warriors using rest stops as free campgrounds. The only times I've ever been removed from a rest stop for – y'know – resting, were in The Badger State. Fortunately, another member of the touring army had a relative who owned a field in the area. We drove along Wisconsin back roads until we arrived at a farm around the Illinois border. That would be as good of a spot as any.

Upon awaking, we then descended upon the University of Illinois campus after a stop at a grocery store. After buying ice for my cooler and another case of Cokes, I had just enough money for parking and my concert ticket. I might have had little money, but I did have over forty sodas. If I got rid of them all, I'd have enough buffer to make it through a few more nights.

The key to selling sodas is to wait for the post show rush. You can vend a few before the show – and usually when I was in crunch mode, I made a point to do so. At a Grateful Dead concert in Buffalo I hawked over 50 drinks before going in – but it's right after where the money can be made. This was especially true in the smaller venues of Phish tour. I just had to be patient and hope things would work out. In the meantime there was a concert to see. That is the point of this endeavor after all.

After all of these theatres and clubs, the 9,500 person capacity UIC Pavilion was a bit of a culture shock. This venue is big enough that Phish returned there in 1998 and again in 2011. Admittedly it was an exceedingly difficult ticket in 2011, as opposed to being able to pick up tickets at the box office, but it was still surprisingly full. I was growing to accept that Phish was playing larger venues in the northeast. That was their home territory. A venue this large in the Midwest was surreal; yes, they played the even larger World Theatre in Tinley Park the year before, but I wasn't there so I hardly think that that counts.

This being my first real Phish arena show, I decided to import a concept from Grateful Dead tour and do some hall dancing. People used to just stalk out a position in the hallways and dance there. When I first started seeing shows, this was so popular that the Grateful Dead put up speakers in the hallway to facilitate fans being able to hear the music. Eventually, the band got into some sort of trouble with those speakers, due to an issue involving the low powered FM transmitters that were used to broadcast the signal. That made it harder to hear in the hallway but didn't stop anyone.

Why would we go out into the hallway where the sound was worse and you couldn't see? It was done to have extra room and also to get away from the annoying subgroups of the crowd that infested the tour once "Touch of Grey" became popular.

It was bad enough that people were able to make money by selling buttons that simply said, "Don't Ask Me For Drugs." Even wearing that, I had to fend off constant requests to sell substances, ones that I wouldn't even take myself. The more you denied it, the more that the other person assumed it was an elaborate way to signal that you were in fact a dealer, but you were trying to stay below the police's attention. Around 1991, I made up a game where I would score a point if someone asked me for drugs at a show, two points if they did so during a set. I made a point of recording them in my setlist notebook after each show. [43]

---

[43] I no longer keep a setlist notebook now that there are reliable online resources, but my Grateful Dead book is amazing. I didn't just record the setlists. I was way too obsessed to think about doing just that. I have the lengths of sets. When I went on tour, I recorded the distance between venues. After Brent Mydland's death, I went back and notated all of his final versions at shows I attended. As if that weren't enough, I then went back through earlier shows and figured out how many times I had seen each song, and wrote that number next to each song. Then I had a sidebar

Hall dancing never was really a thing at Phish. The Phish crowd wasn't nearly as bad. Sure, my all time record score was 31 points at the 1992 Jones Beach H.O.R.D.E. [44] show, but the nature of that festival meant that a lot of people had never heard of most (if not all) of the bands playing and just went for something to do. By the time Phish actually had the reputation for being a party scene, I was old enough that I no longer looked like a good source for chemical enhancement. Even if the crowds had started off bad or the hippie vibes of the Grateful Dead stuck around more at Phish, the real reason why hall dancing never would be a thing at Phish is that the band was too active on stage.

The Grateful Dead were never very visually interesting. At most Bobby might lunge forward at a dramatic moment in a song. Most bands like to have some sort of big entrance. The Dead would come on stage, turn their backs to the audience, fiddle with their instruments, and play brief snippets of songs as a way to suggest to each other what they should open with. Sometimes they'd do this for five minutes before finally turning around and starting a song. Their static nature is the real reason the hall dancing culture evolved. Phish always have the threat of visual spectacle and that is why few ever stayed in the corridors.

However, this night was the experiment. That's where I was during "Divided Sky" at least. That song has a long pause in it. The band tends to freeze in place during it; as one of my standard dances, I would also do the same. For some reason, this night I was in the freeze zone. This was an incredibly long pause, but I was a statue. I actually was having an out of body experience during this moment. It was bizarre but powerful, a memory that stood with me for years.

What makes it even more surreal is that somehow Trey was having a

---

on the right for each show that had the average of those numbers, the difference between that average and the one from the previous show, and "Show/Song." The latter would take the number of the show it was and divide it by the average in an attempt to try to normalize the numbers a bit since the average would obviously go up once I saw more shows. The Phish Stats website was somewhat inevitable.

[44] Standing for Horizons of Rock Developing Everywhere, the initial lineup was the early 90s jambands scene: Phish, Widespread Panic, the Spin Doctors, Blues Traveler, and Aquarium Rescue Unit.

similar experience at the same time. I didn't learn this until years later when he mentioned it in an interview. Even in the infamous 2004 Charlie Rose interview, the one where he was explaining why Phish had to break up, this "Divided Sky" came up:

"We were at the UIC Pavilion in Chicago. And we were playing 'Divided Sky,' and we got down to this quiet part where it gets silent. And we were getting quieter and quieter, and then became silence. And I had my eyes closed, and I could feel the crowd, and I started to — because improvising is, you're trying to translate the — what's out there already, greater pattern of things. And sometimes it feels like it's coming through the hole, and you couldn't play a wrong note if you tried; you're just floating.

"And at that moment, you are in the middle of it, and I started to see these colors, like I'm not kidding, floating around there, and I realized that I could almost — it was silent - but I could see what we were translating. And as soon as I could see them, I started improvising, but I didn't play anything. I did everything in the sense course of improvisation, except for the actual notes, and as soon as I did it, the whole place erupted. [Makes a sound like the crowd cheering] It was like, [makes sound again] and just tears started rolling down my face, and it was at that moment that I knew that it was truly bigger than me. It."

I have no idea if somehow what was happening to Trey affected my moment or what was happening to me pushed Trey over the edge, but there was definitely something in the air in that "Divided Sky." It doesn't translate at all to tape, but I wonder how many other people were having similar experiences during a few minutes, minutes where no actual music was even playing. I have no idea what caused it, but it will always fascinate me.

While the moment I most remember was one where no music was playing, there are some excellent versions this night. What most people think of when 6/18/94 gets mentioned is the "David Bowie," and the "Mind Left Body Jam" in the introduction.

Before there was a Mockingbird Foundation and *The Phish Companion*, there was *DeadBase*. In addition to being an amazing reference tool, *DeadBase* was every obsessive's defense. "Yes, I'm bad," we would tell our families, "but these guys are far more obsessed than we ever could be!" One of my favorite sections of the book was the introduction. In it, John W. Scott would talk about teases and mislabeled tapes. It starts out sanely enough with general observations and research (e.g. Re if there were four shows at Los Angeles' Shrine Auditorium in November 1967, "The evidence for just two shows is stronger: there are only two dates (10th and 11th) on the poster for the shows and only two dates are on the *Anthem of the Sun* album cover"), but there's always that moment, where he reaches his limit. When the 8/27/72 show was mislabeled at 10/24/74, early editions have him saying, "10-24-74? COME ON!" Sure, there's no chance that the Grateful Dead played a concert on October 24 as 10/20/74 was the famed Farewell show – their breakup lasted shorter than Phish's hiatus mind you – but that reaction sums up the nature of the obsessive mind. When you dive deeply in a world like that, it can be hard to remember that other people just occasionally listen to a tape and enjoy the music.

In addition to the correcting of tapes, there were annual debates between the authors. Was it "Aiko Aiko" or "Iko Iko," "Pretty Peggy-O" or "Fennario?" Most heated was that around a little theme the band played. The Dead had a couple of riffs that they used to populate jams in the early 1970s. One of them was just called "Spanish Jam" for the feel that it has. The other one was more controversial. Some thought it sounded like Bob Weir's "Heaven Help the Fool." Scott was committed to it being based on Baron Von Tollbooth and the Chrome Nun's "Your Mind Has Left Your Body."

While Baron Von Tollbooth isn't the most popular band in the history of mankind, they should be better known than they are. The album's lineup is a hodgepodge of the Grateful Dead and Jefferson Airplane. The riff is pretty clearly heard in the introduction of the song, which leads me to think that there was some intentionality there, even if the official Grateful Dead policy seems to be to mock it. When *Dozing At the Knick* included the *'Terrapin* Station" that has that theme, they labeled it "Mud Loves Buddy Jam."

Despite the ribbing of the song title, it seems reasonably possible that Jerry was channeling a song that he had played on, especially since the album was released around the time that theme was first explored. The idea that Phish was intentionally referencing that jam seems much less likely. Regardless of intent, it's a beautiful introduction to "Bowie," a highlight not just of the show, but of the whole tour really. It shouldn't be surprising that it worked so well, after all both Trey and I had the experience earlier that night of our minds leaving our bodies.

Between the weird experience, the beautiful "Bowie," and the fun of the Monty Python "Spam" song being sung in the "You Enjoy Myself" vocal jam, I had completely forgotten about my financial problems. Fortunately UIC would give once again. This venue was three to four times the size of the places they had been playing but there were the same few post-show drink vendors doing the tour. I had slung sodas outside many a concert, working hard to perfect my marketing pitches and avoid security. Never before had I seen an experience quite like this. There were so many parched people that I had to turn away buyers because I didn't have time to make change. Even doing that, I sold out of all of my drinks in less than two minutes.

I was so amused by this, that I asked a fellow vendor if I could grab a couple of Frescas that had been sitting in the back of his car and try to sell those. My sales pitch of "Warm Fresca" tried to make up for its lack of appetizingness with pure honesty. I actually managed to sell a few much to the surprise of everyone involved. It's not often a show has a both a musical peak and a somewhat unrelated mystical experience. Throw in the best vending night in my life, and Chicago was definitely being my kind of town.

18: JUNE 19, 1994 – STATE THEATRE KALAMAZOO, MI

A day between

Some towns are known for being centers of business. Others have landmark buildings or famous sports teams. And then there are the towns that are well known because they have funny names that are amusing to say. Tucumcari, New Mexico and Rancho Cucamonga, California got mentioned in songs. Yreka has a certain amount of fame for having a store with the unlikely palindromic name of Yreka Bakery. Albuquerque isn't just the largest city in New Mexico; it is the place where Bugs Bunny never could remember to turn left. Kalamazoo joins that illustrious club. Everyone vaguely knows that the place exists but few have been there or could find it on a map; my own association with it is from the parody of "Deck The Halls" in the comic strip Pogo, "Deck us all with Boston Charlie/Walla Walla, Wash., an' Kalamazoo!" It still has a better fate than Truth or Consequences, New Mexico, the town that renamed itself for a TV show that has been off the air for decades and now just gets called "T or C" by locals.

When you have a name like Kalamazoo, the one thing you should always be prepared for is questions about its origin. T or C was renamed to win a contest. Walla Walla translates to surprise over how much water was present at that location in the eastern Washington desert. Kalamazoo's etymology is more shrouded. Everyone is pretty sure that it's a Native American term, but what it meant is not known. My personal favorite option is, "the area where animals wounded by Indians crawl to die," but if you asked me on June 19 what I thought the name meant, my most likely definition would have been, "Sorry, we are closed on Sunday."

The one constant from living off the road is that there is a lot of downtime. While tour provides a few unique ways of burning hours such as endless rehashing of previous shows in rest stops and arriving early to the venue so you can try to find an open window that will let you listen to Phish's frequently bizarre soundchecks, that only ameliorates the situation a little. When you're living close to the edge, you have to find ways of passing time without spending what few resources you have. One way doing so is to wander into shops and see what they have. Admittedly, that can quickly become a way of depleting your funds, but it is something to do. Unfortunately, Kalamazoo – at least back in the mid 1990s – was a weekday only town. The Meijer on the outskirts was open, but everything downtown was shuttered. Well almost everything. There was a used bookstore open. I found a copy of an amazing book there: *Bluff Your Way in Math*.

I'm not sure why this book exists. Its purported purpose is to help people who don't know math fake their way through more and more advanced studies. However, making jokes that require graduate level mathematics to get would seem to be playing to a rather limited audience. I'm not aware of teeming multitudes clamoring for riffs on Galois Theory. At least one copy managed to find its targeted audience. On a night where I took I-94 in 1994 to see my 94th show, a little mathematical synchronicity seemed to be in order.

Even more than second night Warfield, this is a forgotten show. On a Sunday night in a small town in Michigan, on a tour surrounded by some of the most famous concerts Phish have ever played, they just came in and performed a concert. "Let's fire up Kalamazoo 94," is a phrase rarely uttered. Once again though, it's a sign of how powerful this year was.

Like so many nights in 1994, where this show picks up is in the "Stash." It starts out with an audience rarity as the cries of "Woo!" drown out the clapping by a wide margin, interesting for those of us wondering about paths not taken. The jam isn't subtle by any means but it's dark and intense and powerful, once again showing off their skill in 1994 of playing with both energy and darkness at the same time.

Phish's second sets usually start off in one of two ways. Either there's a high-energy song to get everyone excited for what's to come or they jump straight into a jam vehicle and start to explore immediately. Kalamazoo tried a completely different approach, leading with "Faht."

"Faht" is a storied song, but only in the literal sense. No one holds up signs for this number or really thinks about it, but the origin of its name is a funny story. The Phish newsletter occasionally had surreal pieces written by band members. Mike's Corner was much more common, but Jon occasionally joined in with "Fish's Forum." One time he was trying to write dialogue with an accent. That can always be dangerous if you're dealing with an editor (or these days autocorrect). The word right in the phrase, "raht tuh the front door," got changed to "Faht." Apparently that incensed Fishman and inspired rants about how the entire meaning of the story was completely ruined.

Around the same time, Jon had written a little number to be included on *A Picture of Nectar*. It starts out with him playing the acoustic guitar, but background sound effects are slowly added. There are birds chirping and woodlands animals and it's peaceful and pleasant but those sounds quickly get drowned out by cars. Lest any calming experience still be had, the song climaxes with a foghorn to drive them away. It was a parody of a certain type of New Age song that was popular – or at least available. Few ever acknowledged buying or listening to these releases - at the time. The label Windham Hill was largely responsible for these atrocities, so Jon named his relaxation destruction exercise "Windham Hell."

Unfortunately for him, he missed the meeting where the album was finalized. Perhaps worried about a lawsuit, the other band members decided it would be best to change the song title. They eventually decided to rename it "Faht," telling Jon that the label made the same mistake as the Fish's Forum editor. A few months after *Nectar*'s release, a heavy metal band in Snoqualmie, Washington formed under the name Windham Hell. While it proved that they didn't have to worry about a lawsuit, at least it prevented a possible confusion. They already had a slight issue being confused with Marillion's frontman Derek William "Fish" Dick; one night at The Chance, I witnessed an angry customer unsuccessfully demanding a refund for his ticket because he was told over the phone that it was the Scottish singer playing there, not a quartet from Vermont. They also didn't need confusion with the Northwest metal scene.

While the backstory is amusing, the song didn't really have a good place in the live setting, largely due to logistical issues. The show would have to stop as Jon came out from his drum kit and grabbed his guitar. As they moved to larger venues, the acoustics of the song worked less. Of course, it also didn't help the cause that the New Age movement acted like the quantum particles they pretended to understand and suddenly vanished. When you could no longer occasionally hear birdcalls mixed with guitar when you shop, the parody didn't work as well. "Faht" was only played 12 times. This would be its second and final 1994 performance. It would appear twice more in 1995 and then become shelved.

The foghorn at the end of the song apparently wasn't just a warning about water vapor in the air. It was also an "Antelope" mating call. The ungulate it inspired to manifest was an impressive specimen indeed; any hunter who nabbed this would gladly mount its head on their wall. The peak is both exceedingly energetic and a little angry.

While there were some very strong versions of songs - "If I Could" is also played with some delicate beauty - and a few interesting song selection calls, perhaps the most interesting moment was the tour's second and final "Makisupa Policeman." This pointed a path towards the future.

According to banter from the 20th anniversary shows in 2003, "Makisupa Policeman" was written in the very late 1960s by a young Tom Marshall. The song is a parody of reggae songs, specifically the marijuana focus. "Woke up in the morning/Smoke a little herb/Woke up in the afternoon..." goes the only verse. Over time the joke about pot's soporific effects got replaced with a celebration of a strain or a random tangent completely unrelated to drugs and policemen whatsoever. When did that start?

It would be cool if I could answer that it first happened at this Kalamazoo show. A completely forgotten concert could have some historic import for the band. Alas that is not true – they sang a variant lyric of, "Woke up in the morning/Policeman in my house/Woke up in the afternoon/Smoke a little herb," which isn't that different from 8/7/93 ("Woke up in the morning/Policeman in the corner/Woke up in the afternoon/Said please don't do that.") or 11/26/90's "Manteca" references ("Woke up in the morning/Crab in my shoe mouth/Woke up in the afternoon/Crab in my shoe mouth."). It appears that the first "keyword" version was six months later in San Diego, "Woke up at 4:20/Smoke the dank." Kalamazoo might not have been the "Makisupa" turning point, but in both lyrics and the style of the jam after the minimal lyrics, it pointed the way towards the song it would become. One foot in the past, one in the future, that's summer 1994 summed up in one song.

19: JUNE 21, 1994 – CINCINNATI MUSIC HALL CINCINNATI, OH

Let me stand next to your…

One side effect of the smart phone era that there aren't any more lost days. We check into places and post pictures. If I had had my phone in 1994, I could tell stories about what I did on the off day between the 'zoo and the 'nati. Maybe I had adventures both epic and world changing. Unfortunately, I have absolutely no idea. I know a book author probably shouldn't admit that, but this was the pre-documentation days. I was living rather than keeping track of what I was doing so I could tell everyone else.

Another thing that's been lost in the era of technology is the ability to pull off ticket scams. Admittedly, I was always the good boy who followed the rules. Well almost always. A few times I skirted around them.

On September 22, 1990 I was stunned to discover that the show at U Mass Amherst was sold out. Who ever heard of a Phish show selling out? It was less bad than a normal shut out as the only difference between being inside the show and outside was what side of a line of the floor you were on. The room opened up into a hallway where you could hear just fine. Still though, it offended me as a matter of principle to not be inside the venue. I had to hatch a plan.

When someone handed me a stub from inside the room, I took it. A security guard turned out to be an ex-Bard student who knew me; she drew a variant of the hand stamp on my pal with a sharpie. I walked to the other side of the room, showed one person the fake hand stamp, got the real stamp on my other hand, went inside… and then ended up spending a lot of the show where I was originally, but I could go inside if I wanted to and that made all of the difference in the world!

That wasn't the only way to get into a show without a valid certificate of entry. Spend enough time on Grateful Dead tour and you learn all sorts of ways to create fake tickets. Sometimes people created fake mail order tickets like the ridiculous cardboard that I was handed outside of the Spectrum on 3/18/93. I was told, "It's fake but it will get you in." Both aspects of that were true. Grateful Dead Tickets sandwiched in extra colorful layers to make their sparkly passes difficult to counterfeit. My Philadelphia fake was twice as thick as a normal one. I'm still stunned it got me into the venue.

Ticketmaster was a much easier target for duplication. The main trick is to get two ticket stubs. You cut off the end of one to make it approximately the size of the stub end of a ticket, tape them together, and use a sharp point to perforate the tape so it rips easily. Different people had different stub collecting techniques. One person I met on summer 1993 used the same stub from the first night of the tour to get in every night. The unquestioned experts of this technique were a group of Deadheads who were known as the Spinners.

The Spinners hated that name. They called themselves the Church of Unlimited Devotion and thought of themselves as a religious group that worshipped the guitar playing of Garcia. The nickname came about from their practice of – you guessed it – spinning in circles when the music played. The reason they didn't get dizzy was that they stared their hands the entire time. If you focus on an object that's moving in the same way as you are, it keeps the side effects at bay. In addition to the rule that they would have to spin during every Jerry led song, they had an all for one attitude. No one would enjoy the show until the entire group got in. In order to make this possible, one Spinner would get a ticket and then pester every single person entering for their stub. They invented a machine that automated the process to turn stubs into new tickets that were real enough to get people into the show. It was actually kind of slick.

Why talk about ticket scamming in the days before bar codes? To this day, there's a theory about this show. Were the events of "The Horse" an innocuous example of Phish fans ignoring the rules that they always blow off or was there a larger plan enacted to get fans into the show? The former is much more likely but the speculation will never will go away.

Even when this show was held, the Cincinnati Music Hall was over a century old. It's a very cool building, built over a mass unmarked grave for victims of a cholera outbreak. Unsurprisingly, there are claims that the building is haunted. Maybe it was ghosts, maybe it was ticketless fans yearning to be inside, or maybe it was the fact that smokers are going to smoke regardless of how often you ask them not to, but a fire alarm went off early in the first set.

A thirty-minute first set that was ended due to sirens would be enough of a footnote for this show, but also interesting was when it happened. When news of *Riff's* track listing first came out, people were intrigued by the fact that there was a song on it that hadn't been played before. What was "The Horse?" It turned out that that was just a name for the first half of what we just labeled simply "Silent in the Morning." While it was a tad disappointing to not actually get a new song, having a label for the first minute is useful. In 1993 that section was often played with Trey on acoustic guitar. Starting on 5/30/93, continuing once in a blue moon throughout Phish's history and then very often in 2013, "Silent in the Morning" was bereft of its equine companion. As much as people might shout out, "'The Horse!' 'The Horse!' My kingdom to hear 'The Horse!'" it didn't appear once the entire year. However, despite the dozen (as of writing of this sentence) "Horseless Silents," our charger always was followed by the appeal for dawn stillness. Always, that is, except for this one time. You want it to be silent in the morning? I'd like that too, but there's a blaring alarm going off and we have to leave the building.

We milled around for a while outside the venue before the fire marshal came around and confirmed that it was just a glitch. Since tickets had already been ripped, anyone who could present a stub at the door was allowed in. The old tricks used to get groups of friends into the same section – walking out with two tickets and handing one to your friend, finding a way of passing it to someone outside quickly usually by putting it in a heavier object and throwing it to them – all of those were valid for entry. I would point out that this might work even today, as a large crowd leaving a building, especially in an age where an attack on one wouldn't be unthinkable, would lead to a quick exit with no time to scan tickets, but I don't want to give people ideas. Even back in 1994, the show was barely allowed to continue. The second set started with a warning that another fire alarm would mean the end of the show. I don't know if the entire audience managed to avoid lighting any plant material on fire for the entire second set, but at least the alarm did not sound and the show went on.

Breaking up the normal structure of the show can be liberating. It freed up the band to try new things. Phish occasionally cover Jimi Hendrix's "Fire," almost always in the encore or second set closing position. The alarm provided inspiration for it to open a set for the first time since 1988. It wasn't just placement that was bizarre on this night. Blacksmiths use fire to improve swords. A fire alarm caused Phish to deliver a much different knife.

"My Friend My Friend" started out pretty normally for a 1994 version, but as the chant of "My friend, my friend, he's got a knife" started, Trey decided to play a riff from Rick Derringer's "Rock and Roll, Hoochie Koo." They went on an excursion that was also akin to Led Zeppelin's "Moby Dick," before finally reminding us that their friend had a knife.

This jam got reprised in the introduction of the following "Split Open and Melt," creating a rather distinct sound. The first minute or two of "Melt" never varies. Throwing in a tease in a place where it's completely unexpected gives it a lot more power. The weirdness continues throughout the jam section of the song. Yes, every "Split Open and Melt" from this summer is a must hear, but this rendition is even better than the 1994 normal. Not only is it the longest version I saw this summer, but it's one of the weirdest. It starts out with the intense jam that was a summer 94 trademark, but the chaos becomes a little too anarchistic to be sustained. The bottom drops out of the music and we're suddenly in a much quieter place. Trey uses the break to build up a melody. Page threatens to call an end to the song by playing the closing riff, but it is not yet time for that. The fire might be controlled but even a spark can still be chaotic. By the eleven-minute mark, they discover a beautiful space, one worthy of staying and exploring for a while. This continues for a while before rebuilding to a peak akin to the jig section of the yet to be written "Guyute," before finally resolving back into "Melt" space.

Sometimes if we get out of our routine in one way, it opens up creativity in other ways. There are many unique versions of songs in this set. The "Chalk

Dust Torture" has a long jam on Heart's "Barracuda" in the middle. Perhaps the oddest arrangement though is what they did to Mike's bizarre pop punk number "Big Black Furry Creature from Mars."

"BBFCFM" is one of the earlier Phish originals. It's unlike any other Phish song, taking its cue more from the Sex Pistols than the progressive, classic rock, or bluegrass roots that so many Phish songs come from. It's a fast, angry song that tells a simple drama. In the first two verses Mike tries to kill the listener. That effort apparently fails because in the third he gives up and just runs away from us. What explains such aberrant behavior? Apparently we are the titular character.

It's a very silly song, rooted in Phish's suburban origins. Punk grew out of a lower class political angst about the artists' lack of economic opportunity and frustration over a power structure that was biased against them. The members of Phish experienced little of that. If they want to tap into existential angst, they had to invent a science fiction scenario in order to do so. There's a fine line between parodying a genre and using its idiom to do something else. Fortunately for Phish here, there actually is a history in the punk movement itself to make sillier songs with the same energy and basic chord structure. The Ramones built an entire career around that. If nothing else, expressing the anger in a silly way is true to who Phish is and that makes it legitimate just by itself. [45]

---

[45] Another great example of Phish taking an activity created out of anger and frustration and channeling it through their life experiences to turn it into something sillier is what happened at the end of the *Quadrophenea* cover show. After playing The Who's classic album on 10/31/95's middle set, they encored with another cover, "My Generation." They played this on different instruments than their usual ones and – taking after the British band – destroyed the guitar and drum kit (with The Who's logo on it) at the end of the song. Instead of doing so out of uncontrolled rage, Trey and Jon were methodical in their actions. They eventually took out a giant cartoon plunger, pushed on the handle, and blew them up. It was silly but as a Phish take on The Who, it completely worked.

If you want a less visual one, 3/1/97 (released as *Slip Stitch and Pass*) referenced "The End" by The Doors. While the original has a dark, pretentious Oedipus complex reference, Phish talks about wanting to cook breakfast for his mother and for her to lend him the car. You have to give Phish credit for staying true to their roots.

This version was different than all others. Between the second and third verses, there's an abrasive instrumental section. After it ends, traditionally Fish counts out "1-2-3-4" and they finish the song. This time, the completion of the noise led to Phish abandoning electricity and moving to the front of the stage to do "Ginseng Sullivan" with no amplification. Then "BBFCFM" was completed. The punk rock song was played on acoustic instruments, only loud enough to be heard if you cupped your ears. It was a different take on the song for sure, but this was a night to break all rules.

20: JUNE 22, 1994 –
VETERANS MEMORIAL AUDITORIUM
COLUMBUS, OH

Save. Your. Life.

The World Wide Web might not have been invented yet, but there was still Usenet for those few hardy folks who already were using it for information. Being the addict that I was, I wanted to read what the greater community thought of the recent shows. There was only one reliable way to get a hookup back then. The Internet was mostly students, leading to frustration at the beginning of each semester as new users arrived and had to be taught the correct rules of behavior. When it hit mainstream popularity (caused in part by AOL allowing connections to the greater community) it was referred to as "Eternal September." The advantage to this is that there was always a way to get connectivity. I drove to the campus of OSU and went to their computer lab.

Technically these labs were only for students but I learned early on in the summer that no one ever checked for student ID. As long as I was able to telnet over to emmy.nmsu.edu [46], I could log into my account and see what important email I had received. Sure it's not quite as efficient as doing so from a cell phone or even a laptop, but there was one true advantage 1994 had that later years didn't: spam didn't exist yet. I was on some very high volume mailing lists, which meant that I did receive 200 emails on some days, but it was all from my extended group of friends. No offers for questionable medicine, no Nigerian scams, all email was wanted at least in theory. Let's just

---

[46] All of the boxes for the department were named after female mathematicians. Emmy was for Emmy Noether, an algebraist known for having Noetherian Rings named after her. A Noetherian Ring is one where every non-empty set of ideals has a maximal element, but I imagine most of you already knew that.

take a second here and mourn the passing of the days when getting email was inherently good.

As email rules were changing, so was the scene outside of shows. Sure there were always a few people seeing multiple shows at a time, but the key word was "few." On 1992's I-64 tour I spent the night at Chez Rest Stop with three other people. Oddly enough, all of us lived in different states that summer but were all moving to New Mexico in the fall. This was my first group of New Mexico friends and we all met in Virginia. There were a few more fellow travelers in 1993, but the entire touring population fit into my Geo Metro for a terrifying March drive along an ice covered US 550 between Gunnison and Phoenix. A person here or there going to many shows in a row is one thing, but by Columbus there were a few dozen. That appalled Brad Sands.

I didn't hear the original comment that inspired this, but the pre-show lot conversation was about how he thought it was lame of us to do nothing but see a rock band over and over again. This led to us making the, "No we're not all losers, Brad" list in which we all detailed who we were and what we did when we weren't seeing endless Phish shows, "Graduate student in mathematics," was my entry. A few years later there would start to be professional tourers, people who just went to shows and did little else. I have to admit that I never have been tempted by that lifestyle. Sure I see a ton of Phish shows – 301 at present writing – but it always is as a form of vacation.

I think it's always important to balance the tour life with the real life. Joni Mitchell has an entire album about the problems that happen when you spend your entire youth drifting and then you suddenly discover that you're no longer quite that young but you know of no other way of living.

Zzyzx Tour Lesson Number Ten: *It's important to follow your bliss but equally important to have a life off of the road. Without that, you're liable to destroy your interest in the band through sheer overexposure and be left with nothing. Tour is a supplement for life, not a replacement.*

As for my tour/life balance, I would have a decision to make after this show. I was only a few more hours away from my family so it was time to stop home for a visit. The only question was when. I could press on for the next four shows and stop in after West Virginia or take those shows off, go home, and see the NC/VA/PA run. It would all come down to the quality of Columbus.

There's a trend in modern Phish thought to think in terms of show quarters by dividing each set in half. That's a legacy of the Grateful Dead days where most of the serious improvisation would happen pre-"Drumz"[47], but Phish can occasionally fall into that pattern too. This isn't to say that the first set of Columbus was a throwaway, but the focus this night will always start on the "2001" and end as "Fluffhead" starts. It doesn't mean that you shouldn't listen to the "Maze" or "If I Could" or "Stash" from the first set – even the least impressive "Stash" of this tour is worth a spin – but the excitement starts later.

The Columbus second set is a cross between the Bomb Factory and O.J. shows. While its centerpiece is a long version of a song in which other tunes are interspliced, it starts out the same way that Milwaukee did: a news update over Phish's cover of Eumir Deodato de Almeida's arrangement of Richard Strauss's "Also Sprach Zarathustra."[48] In this case it was a score update. For basketball fans who were curious about game 7 of the NBA Finals, we were told that the Rockets had a 5 point first quarter lead.

Of all of the things that have changed over these two decades, one of the most dramatic is how much easier it has become to multitask. It used to be a real question if you should stay home from a show if your team was in an important game. Game 5 of the 1995 Yankees/Mariners ALDS was played when Phish was in Missoula. I exchanged banter back and forth with a

---

[47] Starting in the late 1970s, there would be a long drum solo halfway through the second set followed by a long spacey section where everyone but the drummers played. This was referred to as "Drums>Space" or "Drumz" or "DrumZ>Space" if you wanted to be ultra-heady.

[48] If that sentence wasn't confusing enough, consider that Deodato wrote his arrangement for the movie *Being There* but Phish fans always label the track "2001" after the other movie that contains this song, albeit in a much different form. It's still easier than trying to remember how to spell "Zarathustra."

Yankees fan, got an update from CK at the end of the set break (4-2 Yankees at that point), and that's all I could do to keep track of what would turn out to be the best game in Mariners history.

There are nights when I regret that decision. The Missoula show – other than a great "AC/DC Bag" to open and the only "Keyboard Army (reprise)" – didn't offer that much, and the Mariners' comeback was impressive enough to prevent the team from moving to Florida. While I wasn't able to see it live, I do have the memory of getting in my car after the show, turning on the engine, and immediately hearing, "It took 19 years but the Mariners are finally playing in the American League Championship Series." Due to strict attendance rules at my job, I had to drive all night to get back to Seattle and go to work the next day. Fortunately AM radio can travel amazing distances at night. I was able to pick up the flagship station before I even hit Spokane. They didn't want to talk about anything else all night. I must have heard the highlight of Edgar Martinez's double a dozen times.

There's no way I'd ever voluntarily return to a world of information deprival, but there is something to be said about forced suspense. If nothing else, scores that we would never have cared about from the middle of games are forever immortalized. The Rockets were up 5 at some point on 6/22/94, the Bears were up 10-3 over the Cardinals with 5 minutes left in the 3rd in a pre-season football game played on 8/14/93. Trey knew people at the show would want to know and now anyone who listens to the recordings of these amazing concerts will learn these facts. Sure, they belong in a category of knowledge even lower than trivia, but these announcements anchor the concert into a place in history.

While "Also Sprach" eventually became a stretched out jam that sometimes crossed 20 minutes, it started out more humbly. When they first started playing it in on 1993's summer tour, it stuck closely to the popular riff, usually staying between three and four minutes with little extra playing between the two "verses." What it lost in terms of length, it made up with sheer quantity of playing. It opened up the second set of eight of the ten shows between its debut on 7/16/93 and 7/28/93; the only exceptions were the two one set H.O.R.D.E. shows interspersed with the tour. In those the song opened the only set. By Waterloo it had reached the point where I was asking people during the break, "So, what do you think they'll play second?"

Other than the score update, this version was no different. There were a couple plays on the iconic melody and then a drop into "Mike's Song." "Mike's Song" used to be defined by intensity, a hard driving guitar led jam – sometimes accompanied with the band jumping on trampolines as Chris hit the smoke and strobe light buttons – followed by a bombastic phrase. This riff marked the halftime part of the jam. There was a second section – in the mid 90s this began to contain some extensive improvisation away from the "Mike's Song" riff – followed by the repeat of the halftime chords and a descent into whatever song would follow it. The loss of the second half of the "Mike's Song" jam is one of the biggest complaints fans have about modern Phish. To some degree that can be traced all of the way back to Columbus. Much like the 17th, the halftime chords dropped immediately into "Simple" but this time they stayed away for a long time.

This "Simple" is divided into three parts. At first it's just Trey vamping on the riff of the song. While the jam stays in a style of jamming similar to "Simple," it quickly has the theme from the Allman Brothers' "Midnight Rider" become the focus. Playing two songs at once wasn't enough of a trick. To add degrees of difficulty, "Catapult" was then sung on top of the "Simple/Midnight Rider" combination. The theme of the night was merging and melding.

"Simple" returned in earnest after the "Catapult" interlude. This is my personal favorite from the summer. Once they figured out what to do with this song, the focus was largely about the beautiful outro jam that emerged, but in the summer it was all about energy and discovery. The best part about Columbus's arrangement is the saxophone verse. Trey lets out a somewhat evil laugh after "We've got a saxophone," and there's extra yelping and harmonizing all around. There might be an alternate universe that's exactly like ours except that "Simple" never became refined. It would be fascinating to see what would have happened to this song over the course of a few years. My best guess is that it would have dropped out of rotation and been an occasional tune, but we will never know.

As the "cymbop and beebophone" lyrics were sung, it was time to have another song combination. Trey chorded "Icculus" underneath the vocals. "Icculus" is the rarest of the Gamehendge songs. It would only be played four more times in the 90s and then not again until 2009. It's a pretty simple ditty. Trey tells us that we need to read the book (as in *Helping Friendly, The*, the religious text of the people of Gamehendge) in shriller and shriller tones as the same chords underneath the rant get louder and louder. Eventually background vocals come in below the rant, starting out normally enough but rapidly becoming histrionic. The appeal of this song is pure wackiness and on that front Columbus delivered. The highlights are Fishman screaming, "What? You think you're too good for the book," Trey's preaching of, "Save your life. Save. Your. Life. SAVE IT! You might think that your life is OK. You might think that everything is fine. But you are wrong. You are wrong. You're all wrong," and Mike's incredible bass line underneath the peak; if you own the *Live Phish* recording, it's at 2:55 of the track, but it's even more obvious on audience mixes. For fans of the silly Phish, this is as good as it gets.

As "Icculus" winds down, they start wrapping up loose ends. First playing one more pass of "Simple's" first verse, they use that to propel themselves back into "Mike's Song," some 21 minutes after it first started. For a second the show tries to go back into a normal "Mike's Groove" space. "Mike's Song," the instrumental "I am Hydrogen," and "Weekapaug Groove" were played one after the other every time "Mike's Song" was played from 11/5/88 until 12/31/92. The space between "Mike's" and "Weekapaug" opened up to include other songs after that, but for over 200 consecutive appearances, those songs were linked up. Especially for those of us who attended concerts in the days where that was a rule, it always feels right to have them combined. In this case it felt like a restoration of order. They had all sorts of wackiness in the middle of "Mike's Song," but this is tradition. That feeling lasted for seconds into the "Weekapaug" jam.

"Weekapaug Groove," Phish's ode to the beach community of Weekapaug, RI as filtered through the Frankie Valli and the Four Seasons song, "December, 1963 (Oh What a Night)"[49] usually is a high-energy dance tune.

---

[49] Trey explained the story behind the song on 8/10/04. They were driving back from a gig in Weekapaug, "December 1963" came on the radio, and Mike just started singing, "Oh I, trying to make a woman that you move," over the chorus. Even

This time though it got quiet and quickly became another digression: my only "The Man Who Stepped into Yesterday" of the tour.

"TMWSIY" is a delicate instrumental that – for no apparent reason – gets paired with the traditional Yom Kippur prayer of "Avenu Malkenu." "Avenu's" arrangement for Phish is rockified, with power pop choruses and a quick bass tease of "If I Were a Rich Man" from *Fiddler on the Roof* in the middle. Then usually "TMWSIY" is reprised. The combination of delicateness and energy, of an original that sounds timeless combined with an old prayer that sounds recent is a popular pairing. This version brought something extra to the table; a cool digital delay loop akin to the one in the Bomb Factory "Tweezer" made a brief appearance before a sudden drop into "Fluffhead."

While the rest of the show from that point becomes somewhat standard for the tour – of course this being June 1994 means that it all sounds amazing – the first forty-two minutes of the set sealed my decision. It was time to drop off of tour for a few days. It's not like they could top this show any time soon, right?

---

though it doesn't make sense, the words stuck. Most people go through a phase of thinking that it's the more intelligible "Trying to make a woman match your moves," but sometimes Phish lyrics are about the sound they make when they're sung instead of "meaning" and "stories" and "using language to convey ideas."

21: JUNE 29, 1994 –
WALNUT CREEK AMPITHEATRE
RALEIGH, NC

I snost.

There's a phrase that gets used a lot on Phish tour: "You snooze, you lose." Phish have a tendency to reward people who go to small shows in obscure towns. If there's a mid-week show in Boise or Salt Lake City or Las Cruces, there might just be a few surprise rarities to reward those who attend, especially if it is between higher profile concerts. The classic example of this happened in 1998. Phish played two extremely sold out concerts in Las Vegas for Halloween, but the next show in Salt Lake City was half full. As a result they quickly learned *Dark Side of the Moon* as a special treat for those who attended… or as a warning for those who blew it off. Interpretation is up to you.

While the phrase is used extensively – it's especially popular for people who have tickets to an upcoming show that they think might just fit the rules - its origin comes from summer 1994, specifically for the shows that I decided to blow off. I can proudly claim to be one of the first victims of "You snooze, you lose!"

For the first few days of my break I was blissfully ignorant of anything snooze related. I was hanging with the family, taking a reprieve from the road, relaxing and all was good. It was then that I decided to drive to Towson State University to see what I had missed. The first three shows had some painful moments – the first "NICU" since 1992 was played in Pontiac, the first "NO2" perhaps ever (since it was written back in the early 80s, there could have easily been a performance that was just never documented) happened in Cleveland – but I wasn't too devastated. I had seen some incredible music and you can't get to every show. If it had stopped there, that would have been fine. Unfortunately, there was still the show in West Virginia – the second and final (to date) time Phish ever played the state – to go. Phish have a song cycle about the mountainous land of Gamehendge. Apparently the Mountain State would be the perfect place to perform the whole cycle.

Referred to as the "GameHoist" show, Phish played the cycle – complete with narration – in the first set and then performed the album *Hoist* in its entirety (sans the never played live "Riker's Mailbox," but they did at least have a "Split Open and Melt" jam at the end of "Demand" for extra album simulating verisimilitude) for the second set. This night is one of my biggest Phish regrets. I decided early on to handle it maturely. I simply decided that this show just didn't happen. I have never listened to it nor will I normally acknowledge its very existence.

This isn't the only concert I pretend never happened. I was shut out of the Grateful Dead's performance at the Boston Garden on 9/26/91. A friend called me from the venue and told me to drive over there to get a ticket. Unfortunately, I was confused as to which Dunkin' Donuts was the location where I was supposed to meet him and I finally found him minutes after he gave up and sold his ticket to someone else. While I had fun outside the venue, trying to find a way in and getting setlist highlights from those who left early, I missed a show with "Dark Star," "Eyes of the World," "The Other One," and the final "And We Bid You Goodnight." I can't ever let myself hear what I missed. For all I know, the "Dark Star" jam was incredibly sloppy and the Gamehendge narration from West Virginia isn't clever at all, but there are some risks that aren't worth taking.

Phish's rise to large venues happened in stages. They first played sheds[50] in 1992 when they opened for Santana. The experience was a little weird from the Phish perspective – sets were 40 minutes long; the monitors were not optimized for their music; instead of playing to a crowd who knew every

[50] "Sheds" is an industry term for large summer venues with a covered seating area up front and a lawn in the back. When you travel around the country seeing shows in different venues, you start thinking a little like a concert promoter. We aren't professionals but our experience in going to many different venues lets us see pros and cons of arenas and sheds that get missed by people who only go to their local venue and think that that's just how things work.

change in every song, they performed for people who were just killing time waiting for the real band to start – but it enabled them to learn how that experience would work. The following summer saw the first toehold into larger venues as a headlining act, but only in the northeast where the core of their fanbase was. Walnut Creek was a new frontier. This night was their debut as a solo act playing a shed in the southeast.

Perhaps as a result of that, the setlist played it a bit safe. This would be the first time seeing the band most of those in attendance; they had only played Raleigh once before in their entire career, at The Brewery, a 300-person capacity venue. There's a reason why the standard songs are the ones in rotation and rarities are uncommon. Sure it's fun to mix things up to help keep it interesting for people going night after night, but the heavy hitters really are their better songs. This night was a Phish sampler. This is who they were in 1994 and why you should come see them again. You snooze you lose events are horrible to miss if you're doing a tour, but it's shows like this that you play for your friend who is curious about this band you talk about all the time.

What did those seeing their first show hear? Their first song was "The Curtain" which is a damn fine introduction to the band. The "Reba" that followed two songs later was even better, even if I didn't appreciate it at the time. Unfortunately I had an issue with the song.

"Reba" and I started seeing Phish together. My first show was the 6th performance of the song about creating artificial meat. While no tapes circulate, she most likely had a different arrangement; between the second chorus and the composition that we know, there used to be a short metal-esque jam under which "Bag It Tag It" was sung in a bit of a falsetto. The extra section didn't last for long. My second show – 11/16/89 at Pearl Street in Northampton, MA – was the 10th known "Reba," and also the first appearance of the modern arrangement.

You might think that having "Reba" as a new song and seeing the first real version might give me an affinity towards it, but it became the overplayed song for me. Every Phish fan has one of these, the song that they hate much more than anyone else because it seems like they just can't avoid it. "Reba" was a new song and the rotation was a lot more constrained, so it got played a lot. While it didn't appear as often as "Bouncing" (which I saw in 14 straight shows at one point) or some other songs, it was longer than almost any song that had that heavy of a rotation. Versions from 1990-91 varied very little. With shows then being two sets of 50 minutes, a 12-minute song took up a large fraction of the night. Eighteen of my first thirty-two shows had this song, and by 1992 I was over it. That was unfortunate because the jam in this version is extremely cool. It might stay in the structure of "Reba" but it meanders around the theme in interesting ways. It's a great listen for the non-jaded.

Zzyzx Tour Lesson Number Eleven: *Yes, there will be times when you're completely sick of a song. I know people who even hate "Ghost" or "Tweezer" or other popular songs just because they've seen it one time too many. If at all possible, try to keep an open ear to them because they still could surprise you.*

While there are no bustouts this night, that's not to say that Phish didn't play around a little with the setlist. The introduction to "David Bowie" had a quick version of "Catapult." It might not have been in Columbus's league, but it's usually a good sign when Phish break that one out. "I Didn't Know" had Fishman, "In a never before attempted something or other," play his bass drum pedal on his knee, in the manner of someone playing the spoons. A little bit of silliness, a few interesting jams, some high energy, that usually is the formula for a solid first set.

The second set opened with another quasi-rarity. Phish played "Punch You in the Eye," a few times in 1989 before deciding that it wasn't working. A year later they ripped out the music break, extended it, and played it as the instrumental "The Landlady." She appeared 181 times between 1990 and 1992, with her appearing a stunning 95 times in 1991. The rent must have been due quite frequently that year.

Once "PYITE" returned in 1993, the standalone version started to disappear. There would only be five more performances of this tribute to property ownership. There's a feature in the Phish Stats program that lists the most common songs people have not seen. By being played a lot in an era before Phish got big, many fans have this as the most frequently played number that they have not personally witnessed. Those in attendance this night avoided that fate. Sure the brief but intense "Tweezer" and the delicate Page fills in "Life Boy" were quite liable to get people addicted, but I have it on good authority that Phish is really about padding your stats.

David Steinberg

22: JUNE 30, 1994 – CLASSIC AMPITHEATRE RICHMOND, VA

Fourth wall breach

While Walnut Creek was played for the first time ever, the Classic Amphitheater had a concert the previous year as part of the H.O.R.D.E. tour. Unlike 1992's H.O.R.D.E. tour where Phish played every night – all 4 shows, that is- they had but two festival engagements in 1993 the second being in Richmond. July 27, 1993's show is known more for a stunt than the music that was played.

On the first H.O.R.D.E. tour, John Popper and Phish collaborated on a joke. The then massively overweight Blues Traveller harmonicist was given his own trampoline during "You Enjoy Myself." It broke on Popper's first jump. A few months later, John had a motorcycle accident that left him temporarily wheelchair bound. When Phish joined the Richmond rebel H.O.R.D.E., they once again played "YEM." A third trampoline was set up – a large one in this case – and a wheelchair was slowly lowered from the ceiling. As the chair slowly descended, Popper's harmonica joined in with the band in a rather impressive jam. We were wondering how the chair would bounce on the canvas, when the cord suddenly snapped sending the chair through the trampoline. There was then a cacophonous peak followed by the band leaving stage and Popper – actually hidden offstage the whole time – asking for help through his microphone. It was a bizarre ending to the show and one of the first Phish stunts.

Perhaps because the venue had already been played, this concert had a much looser setlist than the night before. Sure the first set fit the pattern of a high-energy performance, with well-performed versions of the compositions anchored around an exceedingly strong "Split Open and Melt;" this

126

performance centered on a raucous repeated three chord phrase that Trey used as a battering ram. As the jam moved towards its conclusion, there was another quick detour. Trey discovers a very fast riff and starts scat singing over top of it. It's an interesting staccato vocal performance, fairly unique in Phish's history and just thrown in the middle of this "Split Open and Melt." The best way of getting over the tendency of Phish fans to whine and complain about repetition is to have powerful and distinct renditions of the song. This was my 10th "Melt" of the summer, and my only issue was that I didn't manage to see even more of them. It's not just that this song would always go to an interesting space. Frequently the subsequent numbers were infected; in this case a little extra menace was added to the "Glide."

"Glide" is a silly little song about how they're glad that we're alive, are joyous that we've arrived but – most of all – are downright ecstatic that we are a glide. This song is known for a few things: Trey and Mike used to slide back and forth on some exercise equipment while playing this in 1992, adding a literal component to the "Glide" title; an early exercise on rec.music.phish as to what fans should call themselves other than the detested "Phish Heads" had "Glides" as a favorite of many; and a disastrous performance of this song at Coventry became Exhibit A for why Phish had to take a break. While the tune is about expressing joy, a defining feature is the mid song break where the riff of the song is somehow twisted to make the bliss Satanic. Happy words turned terrifying is a Phish trademark. After all, they are the band that can creep people out by singing, "La la la la la la/Life is just a bundle of joy."

While Phish had played this venue before, Richmond still wasn't exactly the center of the Phish universe. The second set opened with "Wilson," but the crowd didn't know what they were supposed to do. Towards the end of the extended introduction, eventually a few faint cries of "Wilson" can be heard. Perhaps that was a moment of liberation for the band. They could play whatever they wanted this evening and know that most people would be floored.

It started small. During the introduction of "You Enjoy Myself," a verse and chorus of "Yerushalayim Shel Zahav" was sung. They then returned to the song, but decided to continue vocal shenanigans. The composition has a dramatic build which resolves to a scream. Trey screamed some nonsense over that section, and then added a quick evil laugh. Fishman later voiced some encouragement to Page during his solo, "Yeah! Get it!" Mike gets a similar scream during his turn to shine; even without that, Catcus's solo is a must listen. It's extended and quite inspired.

With all of the vocal antics in the show already, it's not surprising that the vocal jam section of "You Enjoy Myself" is amusing. Trey takes a page out of *The Shining* and starts screaming "Red Rum!" This action continues over the introduction to "Sparkle." The band was clearly in a silly mood and wanted to play games with vocals. That combination leads to only one direction, and that direction begins with an "Oom Pa Pa."

Like in Milwaukee a few weeks prior, "Harpua" was connected to Gamehendge. "Kung" was once more chanted to transport us there; this was the fourth time in two weeks that "Kung" performed this role, but it would never happen again. Then things got weird. The story had Jimmy not be present at home because he was out at a Karaoke bar. A random guest from the audience was pulled onto the stage to sing "Honkey Tonk Women." One might expect a fan's performance to be completely dismal, but they somehow found local musician Sean Hoppe. When he plugged his band's post show event before leaving the stage, it was obvious that he probably was not chosen at random, but the story has never come out. How did Phish learn about Hoppe? Did they plan this song? It sounds too rehearsed to be a random encounter. Did people come out to The Memphis to see The Headstone Circus? June 30, 1994: come for the "Split Open and Melt," "You Enjoy Myself," and "Run Like an Antelope,[51]" stay for the mystery.

---

[51] The "Antelope" is a completely forgotten gem. Between it being in a tour where all versions are amazing and coming directly after a "Harpua," it's easy to overlook it, but it has a "Harpua" tease in the introduction, some fun lyric changes at the end, and a completely intense peak between the two. Just because no one talks about this, doesn't mean that you can't. Be the one who raves about the 6/30/94 "Antelope" before it was cool.

23: JULY 1, 1994 –
THE MANN CENTER FOR
THE PERFORMING ARTS
PHILADELPHIA, PA

The end of an era

If you're traveling from Baltimore to New Mexico and you're in North Carolina, it's suboptimal to head there via Richmond and Philadelphia. My plan though was to maximize the amount of time I spent on the road before having to return to Cruces, and I figured I could just squeeze in one more show.

Philadelphia area shows have a reputation for being sketchy but that is largely due to the venues they play. Camden is a depressing shell of a city, Atlantic City is fascinating but that's just because its decay can be romanticized. Even the massive sports venue of the Spectrum is largely known for being the territory of sheer amounts of nitrous oxide dealers due to a quirk in Philadelphia laws making it exceedingly easy to acquire tanks. My first Philadelphia concert was seeing the Grateful Dead at John F. Kennedy stadium in 1989. The show was very nearly canceled because the stadium was so decrepit that it was actually condemned less than a week following the show; rumors had it that the only reason that it was allowed to happen at all was that authorities were terrified that the fans might riot. Seeing how I walked out of the show to the lovely site and aroma of overturned portapotties, perhaps those fears weren't as ill conceived as the Grateful Dead crowd would like to believe. While the scene devolved further after the camping and vending ban at the end of the summer[52], it was already getting

---

[52] For years leading up to this tour, the Grateful Dead made deals with the venues to allow people to sleep in the parking lots and sell (non-copyrighted) merchandise in order to stay on the road. While the idea was wonderful for making the Dead scene

rough around the edges.

This fits the popular image that some Philadelphians like to cultivate. You have to be tough to spend time here! Those who equate attending a music performance with an act of bravado might not want to be reminded about the Mann Center. There is little sketchy or dirty or urban about this shed in Fairmount Park. If anything, it's rather tranquil.

While the Mann is smaller than Camden's Insert Corporate Name Here Center – I'd put in the current name but by the time this book reaches your hand, it's likely to have changed again – it's quite possible that 14,000 is a saner venue size for 21st century Phish than the 25,000 seats across the river. Maybe the Mann doesn't want them back, maybe there are technical issues with the backstage area or the stage, but this might be an interesting place for Phish to try again.

(**Author's Note:** Between the time of writing and publishing, Phish have announced two shows at the Mann. It was a weird feeling being mad at Phish for doing what I was about to ask them to do.)

While a capacity of 14,000 is on the small side for modern Phish, this still felt like a large place for Phish to play at the time. This was the third straight shed of the tour but it still was barely a week since Columbus. On the western and Midwest leg it felt like Phish was touring with us. It was a trivial matter to talk with band members after a show and they knew the people who were attending every night. If I didn't understand those days were ending, a brief interaction with Mike before the show brought it home.

---

feel like it was more than just a concert, after the success of "Touch of Grey," lots got overwhelmed by people who were just there to check out the scene and maybe score some drugs. Communities didn't understand why people couldn't just see a concert and then leave like other shows. Banning the practice of camping and vending was the attempt at a solution.

Unfortunately, the actual effect was to knock the people who actually obeyed the rules off of tour. The interesting craftspeople faded away why the drug dealers and scammers stayed around. Without the focus of the lot, the sketchiness migrated all throughout the city, making it harder for the police to track. I understand the idea behind this decision, but this is a reason why things got progressively worse as the 90s rolled on.

On the surface it was little different than any other that had happened this summer. I told him that I was bummed that I missed on the two performances of "NICU" and asked if we could get one that night. Typical fan/band interaction even to the point of me doing the clichéd activity of asking for a rarity. There was just one thing that was different. There was a fence between Mike and the crowd and when a few more people wandered in that direction, he saw that he'd have to duck out lest he be overwhelmed. For the most part it was fun watching the band grow from having trouble drawing people to The Chance to mid five figure crowds, but that moment showed that something would be lost too. This night would be my last time interacting with a band member for nearly five years. On the other hand, I did receive that "NICU."

Other than the "NICU" and the previously mentioned encounter with the taper who recorded Cornell, a few things stand out about this show. The "Foam" – while sloppy in parts – gets quieter and quieter until they're barely playing at all. They might suddenly be in venues way too large to play with no amplification, but they found a way to have a similar effect. There's a great Page led section in "It's Ice" and a reprise of the Richmond vocal shenanigans – in this case some scat singing over the peak – in "David Bowie" and a "Harry Hood" filled with delicate beauty. There were a few rarer songs ("TMWSIY," "Tela," and don't forget "NICU" still had that new bustout scent) and a vacuum solo in "Terrapin" that goes on for far longer than it should.

While the show ended with the "Rocky Top" encore, my tour wasn't quite over yet. There was a party for those of us who braved the Midwest section of the tour up in Trenton. Sure that was another 30 miles out of my way, but as the extended ending of Peter Jackson's *Return of the* King showed, an epic adventure needs some closure. Why does this show symbolize the end of an era for me? Because summer 1994 was still a time where a group of fans could throw a party after a Phish show and have Jon show. It was a casual thing, like he was just another attendee at the concert, but the walls were coming up.

I would never begrudge Phish their success. They work hard, try to respect their fans to the best of their ability, and came about their money by making people happy. To the degree that I know them, they seem to be genuinely nice people who deserve good things. Still though, when I reflect on this year, upon the music and the venues, the interactions and the tight knit scene, I would be lying if I didn't occasionally have the longing to return to this tour. You can make a case for 1995 and 1997 having stronger tours musically, but it's highly unlikely the whole experience will ever be equaled.

It's a long drive back to Las Cruces from New Jersey. I woke up early in the morning and headed southwest. When you're on a 40 hour drive, cities start to blend together and become obstacles instead of destinations. You forget about much of the outside world, as your universe becomes a sequence of white lines and green signs. You can occasionally see other fans heading in your direction towards the start of a tour. It's far less likely on the way home. It feels like a stealth activity, like you have some secret that no one else knows about.

The late night freeways tend to be dominated by trucks. Out in rural western Texas in the region where the plains become the desert, I passed an exception. Volkswagen microbuses always bring images of hippies and Deadheads, but those of us in New Mexico had a different association. They were still being made south of the border in the 1990s and were quite popular in Mexico. Even the modern ones had problems accelerating on hills which is why my 3 cylinder Geo Metro could pass the Chihuahua plated vehicle. As I drove by, I read the text he painted on the windows. "WORLD CUP BOUND!"

Soccer's biggest tournament just had a game at the Cotton Bowl in Dallas. Much like me, he probably had a life changing moment at an event that was completely beneath the radar of most Americans. As much fun as it is to be able to gather in virtual communities revolving around shared interests, there's a different joy in feeling like you're one of the few people who knows about this amazing thing. I didn't yet understand the World Cup and what it meant, he probably had no clue about Phish, but we both felt the need to travel great distances to see our obsession.

There once was a time where you'd have to be exceptionally lucky to find something that you loved. You'd have to stumble across it or find someone to initiate you into the world. For me it was a random Bard student from Vermont with a tape of *Junta*, a new school policy, and the desire to support a local band that started me on the path that led me to be driving down Interstate 20 at 3 AM, heading back home with some new memories and some peak experiences that would keep me going for months.

EPILOGUE: OCTOBER 31, 1994 –
GLENS FALLS CIVIC CENTER
GLENS FALLS, NY

Roadtripping for the milestone

Phish had a radio interview before the Richmond show. I was able to listen to it in the lot and hear the announcement. In the wake of the success of playing all of *Hoist* in the second set in Charleston, they would cover a different band's album on Halloween as a musical costume. The album would be chosen by fan vote.

My initial plan was to not attend this concert. This wasn't out of lack of desire. Despite attending twenty-six concerts over the summer and having the incredible time you read about above, I kept following the setlists and managed to acquire a few tapes from the post-Mann tour. I missed another Gamehendge performance at Great Woods. There was the bizarre second set in Big Birch Pavilion where "Wilson" and "Cavern" were merged - starting as "Cavern," then playing "Wilson" to the other song's tempo, and then reprising the "Give the director" section of "Cavern" at the end – and "Big Black Furry Creature From Mars" was played as "Scent of a Mule." There was the "Harpua" at Sugarbush to commemorate comets crashing into Jupiter in which Page was instructed to play his solo as though he were hit in the head with a comet. Twenty-six concerts, some of the best of my entire music career, and I still managed to have regrets.

Still though, it was a long trip to Glens Falls from Las Cruces: 2,212 miles according to Google Maps. I would have to have someone cover some of my lectures and skip a few of my own classes, although if I'm being honest, after I was awarded my Master's Degree between the Bomb Factory and The Wiltern, my interest in continuing on with the PhD program was not particularly strong. There wasn't much keeping me away from a road trip and then pieces fell into place.

First I was offered a pair of tickets to the show. Then I was talking with someone from Chicago on rec.music.phish who had a brand new car and wanted to break it in by driving to Halloween. Perhaps most importantly, I noticed something interesting. To make it to Chicago in time to be able to drive the rest of the way, I'd have to leave on October 28. My trek for my 100th show would leave on the 5th anniversary of my 1st. It was meant to be.

I left Las Cruces in the evening. While the Interstates veer south, there's a good diagonal you can use to get up to the Midwest. US 70 winds northeast, past White Sands National Monument and Alamogordo[53] and into the hills; the sudden shift from desert to mountain forest is quite impressive. The road continues past Roswell – no, I didn't see any aliens there but I did hear a high school football game on the radio, which was my introduction to the Friday Night Lights culture – and finally, 300 miles later, to the punningly named "Texico" and the Texas state line. From there it's not far to Interstate 44 - home to large tolls and a larger McDonald's – and the state of Missouri.

There are certain events that stick in your memory forever. A few of them might be good, but it's usually the disasters where you can remember every detail of where you were and what you were doing. I was in southwestern Missouri a few hours after sunrise listening to an appropriate tape.

For the past two years I had been a DJ for NMSU's radio station. In a town where the only music to make it on the airwaves was the most mainstream possible, the college station took the opposite extreme. You could only play one track from a band per shift. There were albums in heavy, medium, and light rotation to choose from, but the rule was that you couldn't play any song that was the album selection the last three times it was played; there was a chart on the back where you'd list what track number you played. They were going to force everyone outside of their comfort level, but it was a way of learning new artists.

---

[53] This town is not named after a certain bassist for Phish… as far as we know. Maybe they want to make sure that Mike does indeed remember the Alamo!

One of my KRUX discoveries (and an obsession at this time) was Peter Himmelman. He's a mystical Jewish singer/songwriter, who wrote a concept album that is partially based on his beliefs about the afterlife. I was listening to *Skin* shortly after sunrise and the apropos line, "I've been driving for 16 hours," was playing. Just then I received the first warning. The tape deck ate the cassette.

While I was able to salvage the recording, putting in another tape immediately had the same issue. The rest of the trip was to be without music. A long drive where you can't control the music is annoying, but at least I was in a populated area. There was plenty of radio to listen to and I was only 7 hours out of Chicago. It's a manageable situation, or would have been if that weren't just the first symptom. Around 11 AM just outside of Lebanon, MO my car stopped driving. I was able to get it to the shoulder in time, but it would not start back up.

If I had had a cell phone, the next few hours might have been different. I would have called for a tow and could have been back on the road. But as it was, I had to wait for a cop to show up. He was able to call for a tow truck that took me to a local service station. They were able to quickly diagnose the problem as an alternator but since it was now 11:55 on a Saturday and they closed at noon on that day, they wouldn't be able to get to it until Monday.

The one advantage of being trapped in the middle of nowhere is that it simplifies decisions. My alternatives were to find a hotel room in Lebanon and spend two mind numbing days there or to figure out a way to get to Chicago. Fortunately Greyhound does stop there. It took seven hours until the bus picked me up and about twelve hours to get to the Windy City once it did; the reason the bus stopped at Lebanon is because it stopped just about everywhere. A phone call to my ride had our meeting place moved to the Chicago Greyhound station. We were back in business!

Zzyzx Tour Lesson Number Twelve: *Build some buffer into your schedule. I know this isn't a popular idea in a culture that believes in waiting until the last second to do anything, but going on the road exposes you to all sorts of possibilities. "The highway is*

for gamblers," sang Bob Dylan, and I always am a fan of at least trying to hedge my bets.
Usually it means that I'm just arrive at events insanely early and people make fun of me,
but every now and then this personality trait comes in handy.

All of the insanity meant that we arrived to the venue around the time
doors opened. I barely had a chance to wander around the Civic Center
before it was time to go in. I was able to notice the sign that showed to me
that the scene had irreparably changed. There were tons of people outside
looking for tickets. Phish shows had sold out in the past before – 12/31/91
where I received a pity guest list from then tour manager Andrew Fishback is
the most prominent example, but it happened on a few other occasions – but
there were rarely more than a few extra people trying to get in. This was more
like what was happening at Grateful Dead shows. The secret was officially
out.

The growth of the Phish scene sometimes gets blamed on the death of
Jerry Garcia the following summer, but it really happened in 1994. We went
from a world where Page could casually play a game of pool at Trax before a
show to selling out Madison Square Garden in a little over two years. Until
this year Phish's growth was a long slow process, from bars to larger bars,
from larger bars to theatres, each step playing off of the last. 1994 was the
year where that hard work paid off and a huge leap happened. As impossible
as it would have seemed just a few months prior, the days of theatres were
over.

There was a swap meet at the door. Phish had a scheduled giveaway of
chocolate coins with the Phish logo pressed into them. Normally the trick or
treating convention requires that candy be handed over with no expectation
of a return. Security had their own methodology. In exchange for our
delicious treat, they confiscated anything that could possibly be used
somehow to cause damage to another person. This would be annoying
enough at a normal show, but the Halloween factor caused people to lose
parts of their costume. That didn't happen to me, but this was the one night
where I was not allowed to bring my clipboard into the show. I guess I could
bop someone over the head with it or something.

Since Phish have started covering albums, the Halloween focus has always been on the second set. The first two years had extra tension as they had not yet decided to hand out a *Phishbill*. Starting in 1996, a brief booklet parodying the Broadway publication *Playbill* would be distributed to all attendees. This contained essays as to why the album was chosen along with fake advertisements. The only downside to this was that speculation stopped as soon as the circular was received. It was nice to know the rationale but it came at the expense of surprise. Without it, people were discussing the possibilities all the way through the break.

While the theorizing is always about the album, it can be the first sets that define the nature of the Halloween spirit. The "Harpua" from this night started a running theme of using a narration to talk about the evil nature of Halloween.

The joke was to twist one of their songs to make them evil. 1995 had a version of "Icculus" where *The Helping Friendly Book* wasn't powerful enough to defeat evil spirits, "The book is getting its ass kicked," screamed Trey. 1996 had the Famous Mockingbird replaced with the Killing Death Famous Mockingbird that pecks out Colonel Forbin's eyeballs and then just abandons the quest. This year's revolved around another one of Phish's quasi-songs "The Vibration of Life." Seven beats per second. If you believe the banter Trey recites over it, this pattern has some mystical powers of rejuvenation. Well at least that's normally true. On Halloween everything changes. "The Vibration of Life" becomes a vibration of death that destroys everything in its path.

No *Phishbill*, no idea what to expect or even what genre was likely to be covered, the lights going out for the second set brought a lot of anticipation. A heartbeat could be heard and then a cash register. Some laughing and then a scream, "Aaaaaaah. Aaaaaaaah. Aaaaaaaaah!" *Dark Side of the Moon!* Just as the opening chords of "Breathe" were about to be played, the PA suddenly dropped out. The recording was replaced with Ed Sullivan introducing The Beatles. *Dark Side* was just a fake out; we were going back to the U.S.S.R. for *The White Album.*

Perhaps due to the sheer number of songs on this double album, Phish largely played their version similarly to the original. There were some notable exceptions to that – the "Fool on the Hill" references in "Glass Onion" were replaced with call outs to the then brand new "Guyute," "Rocky Raccoon" swapped a gender to sing, "Everyone knew him as Nancy" in honor of Richard "Nancy" Wright[54], "Don't Pass Me By" was sped up to become a bluegrass track, "Birthday" was played as an instrumental – but for the most part, the costume was as close to the Fab Four's as possible. It turns out that this might have been a good thing for the audience.

As much fun as this set was, there seemed to be a universal reaction to it. People were getting tired of it towards the end. Phish have played longer sets that still left people wanting more. It wasn't the length of the music involved here, but rather the sheer unfamiliarity of it. While the majority of people in attendance owned *The White Album*, the stretch between the Revolutions on side 4 aren't the most popular tunes. Between many songs that people didn't know and the fact that they were all being rearranged for Phish, there was a lot more work required from the audience. When Phish is playing – say – "Bouncing Around the Room," fans know what to expect and they can let their focus slide for a bit. Listening to a once in a lifetime performance means that people are going to want to try to soak in every detail. As much fun as that is, it can also become exhausting.

"Revolution 9" finally arrived. How would Phish reproduce a mélange of studio effects and found audio in a live setting? They resorted to an old trick. The backwards-masking effects were simulated by Fishman playing the vacuum. Everything else was just chanted. But then came the epic moment. Fishman said, "If you become naked," and couldn't resist a first hand demonstration of what would happen.

There is a history of Jon eschewing clothes on stage. The first New Year's Show was billed as "Creative formal dress requested" and had three of the four band members wearing tuxes. Jon opted for a top hat and a g-string. One of my all time favorite rumors, one that I'm afraid to investigate because it

---

[54] Nancy was the author of early Phish songs "I Didn't Know" and "Halley's Comet." Even though he wrote and recorded them, these are usually thought of as originals as the tracks were unavailable until *The Phish Companion* released them as a bonus CD to early pre-orders.

might turn out to be false, is that at a very early Halloween show Jon's costume was an elephant: grey body paint, elephant ears on his hips, and nothing else. Shucking the dress – Jon was wearing more of a housewife dress than his normal frock; Brad Sands wore that. We know that because he came out during "Birthday" to receive a cake since it actually was his – wasn't an incredible surprise but still was amusing. Knowing that this couldn't be topped, they didn't even play "Goodnight." The Beatles' version was played over the PA system as the second set break started.

Third sets on Halloween can sometimes be epic affairs. 1995 had a 40-minute version of "You Enjoy Myself." The following year featured guests from the *Remain in Light* set adding texture to the performance. 1998 was one of the most controversial pieces of music Phish have ever played, centering around a long divisive version of "Wolfman's Brother" and a short "Ghost" where Trey just walked off stage as the jam was beginning. Nothing like that was present at the Civic Center. Phish played a solid series of songs, with a sweet "Slave" and an intense "Antelope," but the memories of the show are of the "Harpua," and my first "Simple" with the modern arrangement – I was hanging out with some fellow members of the #Phish IRC[55] channel and exclaimed, "It's a real song now!" - and the whole concept of the Halloween album, complete with fakeout.

This was a very long concert. We didn't get outside until 3 AM. After a quick nap in a hotel, it was time to reverse my steps. Drive to Chicago, get on a Greyhound, take it to Lebanon and pick up my now repaired car. I tried a different route home, swinging by Carlsbad and the Guadalupe Mountains. US 62/180 is an exceedingly isolated road, passing through endless miles of ranches with nary a town – or even a crossroad – to break up the monotony. It perhaps wasn't the best route when dependent on the radio for entertainment, but the whole experience was worth it for the sudden contrast. After 150 miles of absolute nothing, you go around some curves, down a hill, and you're suddenly in El Paso, a city of a half million people.

That's what Phish in 1994 was like. Four months prior I was seeing them in

---

[55] Short for Internet Relay Chat, IRC was an early Internet gathering place. It still exists today, but its heyday as a place to talk with like-minded people on "channels" for an interest has long since passed.

half empty theatres. Two months later there would be back to back sell out of Madison Square and Boston Gardens. The music might still improve – 1995 and 1997 are largely considered to be the best years of Phish – but 1994 is perhaps the most important year in Phish's history, the year where they made it out of the wilderness.

David Steinberg

ABOUT THE AUTHOR

David Steinberg has been seeing Phish since 1989. He graduated from New Mexico State University with a Masters' Degree in mathematics and used that knowledge to create the Phish Stats website.

In addition to that, he also was a writer for jambands.com since 1998 and was an occasional contributor for *Deadbase*. As a Jewish mathematician, his flare for obsessiveness comes naturally. Yes, indeed, he blames the system!

David currently lives in Seattle with his wife Melissa, and some feline companions. None of them are named Poster Nutbag, and none will ever be. Don't go there.

Made in the USA
Lexington, KY
04 December 2016